We Dare to Dream of an Island of Equals

'For anyone interested in Irish history, politics, trades unionism, music, poetry and storytelling, this is a must-have book. Keep it to hand, preferably on a bedside table, to consult, to browse and to enjoy. Written by the well-known author and traditional musician Des Geraghty, it gives us an insight into the birth of our nation and the part his family played in bringing this about. It covers a wide canvas and is written in a very personal tone. There is something in it to inform and amuse all tastes.'

Mairín Johnston, social activist

'Moving effortlessly from the intimate to the rollicking, from the historical to the anecdotal, this is a panorama of Dublin life like none other, seen with a "pityin' scornin' eye", as Yeats has it in a ballad, a portrait gallery of known and unknown characters, their antics, friendships, conflicts and dreams.'

Gabriel Rosenstock, leading Irish poet, playwright and author

'*We Dare to Dream* could be a companion to Sean O'Casey's autobiographies. It's an important book, which flows from Des Geraghty's strong mother, Lily O'Neill; and woven through his family history is the struggle for workers' rights in the face of powerful employers and a conservative Church and State. It is also the history of the Irish trade union movement and its connections in Britain and the USA. Des and his four brothers came to hold important positions in trade unions. As Des says, many battles have been won, "But we have many more hills to climb ... to create that Island of Equals that our family of seven – and so many others – dare to dream of."'

Shivaun O'Casey, writer and theatre producer

'Des Geraghty tells the story of Dublin working-class radicalism over the past century through the unique lens of his own family, none of whom was willing to be "a mere observer of change". They were in the thick of every battle for justice from the 1913 Lockout to Marriage Equality, and Des is a born storyteller, punctuating his tale with poetry and song.'

Padraig Yeates, historian

'Lifelong trade unionist Des Geraghty has written a fascinating account of growing up in Dublin's impoverished and fast-disappearing Liberties, the intense conservatism of successive Irish governments and the smothering domination of the Catholic Church at the time. He recalls the beginnings of a new radicalism in the 1960s, inspired by the Anti-Apartheid movement and the Civil Rights and Anti-Vietnam War campaigns in the US. He describes the growth of the Women's Movement, challenging a level of oppression scarcely believable today. And all along, he intersperses the story with tales of his much-loved traditional music and ballads.'

Michael Farrell, lawyer and civil rights activist

We Dare to Dream
of an Island of Equals

DES GERAGHTY

Published by
Red Stripe Press

an imprint of
Orpen Press
Upper Floor, Unit B3
Hume Centre
Hume Avenue
Park West Industrial Estate
Dublin 12
Ireland

email: info@orpenpress.com
www.orpenpress.com

© Des Geraghty, 2021

Paperback ISBN 978-1-78605-144-8
ePub ISBN 978-1-78605-145-5

Printed in Dublin by SPRINTprint Ltd

To the late Lily O'Neill and Tom Geraghty, my proud and loving parents; and all those other parents who often have so little yet somehow manage to give our world so much; also my three daughters, Maeve, Nóra and Eva, and their children, who I hope have inherited a better Ireland.

About the Author

Des Geraghty, a proud son of Dublin's Liberties, is a former President of SIPTU and an Industrial Secretary of the ITGWU, a member of the Executive Council of the Irish Congress of Trade Unions and a former Member of the European Parliament. He is currently a member of the Board of TG4 and Chair of the Clé Club (a traditional music club based in Liberty Hall). He is a former chair of the Affordable Homes Partnership and of Poetry Ireland. He has represented the trade union movement on such national bodies as the National Economic and Social Council, the National Competitiveness Council and FÁS. He is a former member of the Board of RTE, ESB Networks and was an elected member of the shareholders of the Abbey Theatre. From 2010 to 2019 he was a board member of the Central Bank of Ireland.

Des Geraghty has participated in the making of many Irish TV and radio documentaries, is the author of *Luke Kelly: A Memoir* and, with photographer Liam Blake, *40 Shades of Green*; he also co-authored the book *European Works Councils: Information and Consultation Rights* with Norbert Gallagher, for the Irish Productivity Council.

Des is also a musician and folklorist and since retiring from SIPTU he has written, directed and performed in a number of music, song and poetry productions in both English and Irish.

Foreword

All my life in Dublin I have been hearing the phrase *everyone has a book in them.* Dublin being Dublin, the rejoinder is often *and that's where it should stay.* Gratitude so, that Des Geraghty has taken up his pen to commit to the record a deeply cultured and complex remembrance of his times past. Not that this is his first venture into print: as well as works concerned with industrial relations and the rights of workers, he's also the author of a bestselling memoir of that other revolutionary Dublin man, Luke Kelly, and of a take on the changing face of the Irish and the changing colour of that face in *40 Shades of Green*, with the photographer Liam Blake.

Born and bred in the Liberties of Dublin, he stands strong on that foundation – and strong, too, in the values bestowed by that childhood, by the hard graft of his parents, by the people of little property and none, by the hustlers, the singers, the musicians, the storytellers, all the teeming life of those streets and their histories.

His mother, Lily O'Neill, emerges from these pages as a profound influence. We meet her first as a teenager, pushing a pram to collect papers from the train at Westland Row, dodging the slimy hands and roaming fingers of a sleazy station porter, to deliver them to her mother, who has the newspaper pitch at the Ballast Office on the quays at O'Connell Bridge. A Communist Party member in her well-spent youth and a woman of deep and wide reading, Lily's curiosity, her courage and her wisdom shine through these memories. With siblings on both sides involved, within her family we have in microcosm the trauma and drama of the Civil War that so divided the country.

Later, as wife and mother, living above her husband Tom's job in Number 3, Cornmarket, and later still in the suburb of Drimnagh, we witness how Lily distilled her passionate politics in the rearing of five sons, all of whom would become involved in movements for social change, for justice, for the building up of communities.

In 2005 Des Geraghty, who clearly adored his mother, penned a gorgeous song for her: 'Lily Bright':

But the landlord calls when there's rent to pay,
The baker sells his bread each day,
The merchant's coal is burning grey,
As you sell the morning papers,
Carrying tales of glorious wars,
Battles fought for every cause,
Where the poor do all the dying.

His father, Tom, home from England, where he had been a young emigrant, met his Lily at the Workers' College and in Connolly House. One of the gifts of this book is how Des Geraghty draws attention to those radical working-class youngsters in the thirties who resisted the threat of the fascist Blueshirts. It is hard now, with hindsight, to credit just how immanent the overthrow of the 1933 elections felt to those on the ground. The enshrining of Des's parents' memory and experiences through the thirties and the forties sheds a deal of light on how it actually *felt* to be young and concerned in the young republic.

We have here, besides, an affectionate and shrewd portrait of Des Geraghty's childhood in one of the oldest parts of the city, and of its community; he is a man formed by that community, a man steeped in the politics of the left, a career trade unionist, a man extremely well placed to chart and memorialise every campaign for the amelioration of the situation of the disadvantaged and for the advancement of egalitarian values – from the struggle for a minimum wage and the forty-hour week, to equal pay, to nuclear disarmament, to the protests against the Vietnam War, to the struggle for human rights for women. The cultural–political lens is especially strong on bohemian life in and around Baggotonia – how the traditional music, the folk music, the emerging rock and roll and the arts as a whole fed into radical politics. The sixties saw painters, poets, singers, players channel and express the aspirations for change; Des Geraghty rightly points to the struggles that gave us, in large part, some of the liberties we now enjoy.

Part family history, part meditation on the State (and state) of Ireland since its foundation, this memoir is also an essential witness to the deep fractures in our culture. It challenges us, especially those of us who consider ourselves radicals, to face these rifts and to find a way through. One shocking statistic Des Geraghty gives us is that membership of the Irish Transport and General Workers' Union (ITGWU) fell from 100,000 to 16,000 after the Jim Larkin–William O'Brien split of 1923, just at a moment when organised labour was the main hope for social amelioration. As he points out, that disastrous split was prophetic of how continuing fractures on the left would hand power in the State first to the Church and latterly, even unto today, to the conmen of the neo-cons. We joke that the first item on the agenda of any radical group is the split, but that mind frame and the continuing fragmentation of a united resistance to late capitalism has robbed us of many opportunities to hold the line against the complete betrayal of the vulnerable in our communities. While we no longer live in a theocracy, and we have marriage equality and we have repealed the insidious Eighth Amendment to the Constitution, with its denial of bodily autonomy to women, we have a huge distance to travel before the vision of James Connolly, the acknowledged tutelary spirit of this book, becomes manifest in a fair and just society. A case in point: the plight of the homeless, which led to Dublin Housing Action movement of the 1960s, vividly evoked by Des Geraghty, is even worse now as we hand the country over to a new gang of ruthless exploiters and their lackeys.

Des Geraghty writes of his native city, from the docks to the mountains, of its rivers and parks, its churches and canals, its granite pavements and its concreted roads, with a deep and wide-eyed affection born of concern and curiosity; but above all else it is his love of Dubliners that energises this work – the people of his city, often flawed, sometimes majestic, sometimes demented, where sometimes the only thing they had of value was their very characters.

There are serious matters here, matters of national import you might say, and Des Geraghty writes of them lucidly and with insight. Equally, he offers a crystal-clear portrait of a unique family, all in their different ways driven by a passion for social justice. That said, this is a joyous book, crammed full with humour, anecdotes, songs, recriminations and harum-scarum carry-on. As full of life and a passion for life as the author himself.

Paula Meehan

Acknowledgements

Thank you to my last surviving brother, Tom Geraghty, with whom I have shared so many happy memories; my partner, Rosheen Callender, and my daughter Eva Geraghty, who both assisted with editing and proof-reading; my friends John Curran, Brendan Byrne, Mick O'Connor, Jack Gannon, Brian Brady and Aoife Brady who gave me ideas, information and inspiration; and Michael Brennan (Director and Commissioning Editor) and the excellent editorial staff (Eileen O'Brien, Benil Shah) at Red Stripe Press, along with Jane Rodgers, freelance editor.

Contents

Preface

An Island of Equals

Once we were seven sturdy roots in stubborn city soil. Our family consisted of two hard-working parents, Tom and Lily, plus five hardy boys: Seán, Tom, Séamus, Desmond and Hugh. All were well nourished on potatoes, porridge, native pride and a strong sprinkling of rebellion.

Our home was in Number 3, Cornmarket, at the top of the Forty Steps, above the old city wall and Saint Audoen's Arch. It was in the immediate presence of two impressive churches of different vintages and different persuasions. The oldest of the two is the medieval Church of Ireland Saint Audoen's, overshadowed by the monstrous stone-pillared Saint Audoen's Catholic Church on High Street. In the older Protestant church, there is a beautiful stained-glass window, dated 1848, portraying the Three Castles of Dublin Corporation. This church provided the chaplains for the Lord Mayor of the Protestant city until the end of the nineteenth century.

The proximity and relative size of these buildings are a statement in themselves, of the centuries-old tensions and competition for visibility and hegemony between these two institutions in the centre of Dublin city. The spiritual needs of the community in that area were catered for more than adequately. There were two Protestant cathedrals, Christ Church and Saint Patrick's, within easy walking distance. There was Michael and John's Catholic Church (Mickey and Jack's, as we called it), home of the famous Smock Alley Theatre on the quays. There were four other Catholic churches: the Franciscan Adam and Eve's, even closer to us; John's Lane Augustinian Church, with its soaring steeple, in Thomas Street; Saint Nicolas of Myra Church in the middle of Francis Street; and Meath Street Church, a few short steps from Thomas Street.

It's perhaps no harm to mention that the populace could also get a penny dinner from the nuns in Meath Street; or earlier, across the road, they could have the benefit of the oldest crèche in Dublin, provided by the Quakers.

The ancient, long-decommissioned graveyard of the older Saint Audoen's Church was our playground park, where we rolled amid the tall grass, the buttercups, the jinney joes, the daffodils and the daisies. Or, if we were making mischief, we might resort to the more forbidding and rugged 'grass yards' of waste ground and old ruined buildings behind the remaining houses of Cornmarket.

One of those houses had a plaque identifying it as Napper Tandy's house – Napper Tandy being one of the founders of the United Irishmen – while two of them, at ground floor level, housed the office and warehouse of James Huggard and Sons. This was where my father, Tom, worked as a storeman for over twenty-three years. We lived there, over the store. So did another family on the top floor, along with the odd individual tenant who might drop in from time to time. Most of the houses were old, decaying tenements. Some had closed front doors; all were well past their better days of municipal glory.

Although this was undoubtedly a disadvantaged area of the city, we found it a rich and rewarding place to grow up in. When we lived there we knew from an early age that this thoroughfare had been trodden by such notables as Zozimus, the balladeer of old; Dean Swift, world-famous writer and satirist; P.J. McCall, traditional musician, folklorist and song writer; James Clarence Mangan, poet and Young Irelander; and Robert Emmet and Lord Edward FitzGerald, United Irishmen patriots and martyrs. For the most part, though, it was the home of decent hard-working people; the men when they could earn a shilling, and the women who were always working to protect their children or to keep the wolf from the door.

In the last century, the area had been very familiar to James Connolly, Arthur Griffith, W.T. Cosgrave and many more. We knew also that this was the home of some great musicians and singers of our genera-tion, among them Tommy Potts, master fiddler; Seán Potts and family; Tommy Reck the great uilleann piper; the Furey family, Travellers and musicians, who lived behind us on Cooks' Street; Leo Rowsome, King of the Pipers; and the home of traditional music and song, the Pipers Club in Thomas Street. P.J McCall, writer of many rebel songs, lived in the shadow of St Patrick's Cathedral in Patrick's Street.

Special friends, to this day, were Mick O'Connor and all the O'Connor family, noted traditional musicians, who originally came from Gray Street; Seán and James Keane, wonderful musicians who went, as did Mick O'Connor, to Francis Street School; and Máirín Johnson, singer and socialist and writer, from close to them in Pimlico, beside the Coombe. We also knew the Potts family well, from Tommy, former fireman and master fiddle player, to Seán, of The Chieftains, and his family. In more recent times Tony MacMahon, the great Clare musician and close friend of Des, adopted the Liberties as his home away from home. Every corner of the Liberties is laden with history – with dark shadows from the past, but also with brighter memories from more recent times. Even in our own home, there were echoes of ancient glory extending back to the Gaelic orders. McGeraghty was one of the four Royal Chieftains of Connaught under the O'Connor kings in the eleventh and twelfth centuries. Another Geraghty was at one time a powerful Gaelic bishop of County Roscommon. The Geraghty family claimed guardianship of the historic Saint Patrick's Bell over many centuries; although my mother remarked that the crack in it wouldn't recommend them for guardianship of such a priceless item.

I thought ruefully of the struggle our parents had to put meat on our table when I discovered that our ancient forefather, the McGeraghty of Connaught, had a personal allocation of 'twelve score milch cows, twelve score sheep and twelve score cows' from the Royal O'Connor King of Connaught.

Lily's family, the O'Neills, were from City Quay. But earlier they were of Wicklow mountain origin, as my mother claimed, since the

O'Neill and O'Donnell princes had escaped from Dublin Castle. Those rebel fugitives were rescued and taken in by the O'Byrnes and O'Tooles in Ballinglen, in the south of the county. Until very recent times, Ballinglen was where Lily's eldest brother Séamus lived with older relatives.

In writing this book, I also discovered that Séamus, Lily's eldest brother, was married to a close relative of P. J. McCall, the writer from the Liberties who composed so many of our rebel songs, particularly from the 1798 period of the United Irishmen in Wexford. Throughout their lives, Séamus and his wife, Brigid, sustained the rebel traditions of their noble antecedents, as did both our parents, Lily and Tom.

This book is both a personal and a family memoir, perhaps subjective and somewhat impressionistic, but a genuine journey down memory lane. It's concerned with the first hundred years of our country as a state, along with some brief thoughts on what we might have to face over the next hundred years. It's more a story from the heart than another lesson in history. In my view, our turbulent history is something that has been catered for very well by recent Irish historians, if not by those in the earlier years of the state.

Given the closeness and somewhat unusual nature of my family, as we all gravitated to trade unionism and Larkinism, I have considered some of our collective experiences and responses to certain important events in our lives, including both disappointments and achievements. We were very different in personality and character, but none of us was willing to be just a mere observer of change. Each of us shared the hope that we might, in some small way, be architects of the future, rather than passive prisoners of our past.

James Connolly, the great labour leader, predicted with remarkable foresight that the division of this country would 'create a carnival of reaction', and indeed it did. It spawned a civil war that had many damaging and long-term consequences. It facilitated the creation of two sectarian states, both far removed from the hopes and aspirations of the common people and particularly those who embraced the whole spirit of an egalitarian republicanism of liberty, equality and fraternity to be shared by Catholics, Protestants and Dissenters of whatever persuasion.

Nevertheless, I hope this story might in a small way celebrate the resilience of our people, who have always refused to be mere victims of repression and injustice. It's also a story of how the women of Ireland have asserted themselves strongly, especially in recent decades, and have, not for the first time, raised us all up. They are, and have been, central to the transformation of our society, hopefully making it more caring and more equal as we continue to journey on our rocky road.

Unfortunately, we lost many great people in the struggle for independence and during the Civil War. We lost many thousands more since then, in an almost continuous flood of emigration. In spite of all these losses, we have retained a strong sense of community, and not a little solidarity too.

I also believe that the vast majority of our people now have the self-confidence and generosity to embrace the 'new Irish' as an increasingly valuable part of our society. Yet we do have a distance to travel to fully embrace all the most needy in our country, such as the homeless and, particularly, our native Traveller community.

On my journey along the rocky road of life, I have had the constant companionship of music, song and poetry. The spirit of these gifts is constantly felt, rather than seen or heard, but is always there, an inherited wealth of priceless riches which is there for all the people of our society to share. I firmly believe everyone has music, song and poetry in their hearts, although not everyone might get the opportunity to express them, and so, very often, they rely on others better able to express these inner feelings for them.

Both my parents and three of my brothers have now departed this life, but their memory still resonates with me and in the hearts of all who were privileged to have known them. Only my brother Tom and I remain to speak or sing their praise.

This book is a small contribution, only a very small part, of their story. I hope that some of the issues remembered will serve to indicate how far we have travelled and how much further we need to go in working towards making our beloved land a genuine Island of Equals.

Des Geraghty, 2021

1

Lily Bright

Oh Lily bright, Oh Lily fair, young Lily of the curling hair
So wan you look in the grey-cold air, selling the morning
papers
Childhood days have flown away, for you the street is school
each day
Chasing pence the game you play, For the men have all
gone marching …
Marching to the drums of war, echoing loudly near and far,
where brave young hearts are beating.
Some have heard James Connolly's call,
Neath the starry plough they'll give their all
Others will follow a flag of green, but more will die for King
and Queen,
On far off fields they've ne'er seen, a cause for which they
never dreamed,
where young red blood is flowing …

Young Lily O'Neill was pushing the creaky old pram down Pearse Street en route to Westland Row railway station. It was very early in the morning and the streets were almost empty, except for stray dogs and a few unfortunates sleeping rough in doorways. She was feeling the cold wet wind through her flimsy dress and threadbare cardigan.

She entertained herself by humming snatches of verses to the scratchy rhythm of the old pram wheels scraping along the cobbled pavement.

See the robbers passing by, passing by, see the robbers passing by, my fair lady, stole me watch an' stole me chain, stole me chain, in Bow lane, in Bow lane, stole me watch an' stole me chain, my fair lady ...

Sometimes she would revert to a livelier rhyme of her childhood days, sung with other children on the steps of Liberty Hall:

Come on an' join, come on an' join, come on an' join Jem Larkin's Union, where ye get yer tay an' sugar free, an' a belt of a baton from the DMP [Dublin Metropolitan Police]. Come on an' join, come on an' join ...

These early morning trips to the station were always uncomfortable, as the summer sun rarely embraced the Dublin streets until much later in the day, while the grey early morning mist was frequently followed by drizzly rain or a bitterly cold wind. Her mission this morning was to collect a bundle of English newspapers and magazines from the early mail train, to be delivered to the Ballast Office at the corner of Westmoreland Street and Aston Quay, where her mother had her newspaper stand.

This was vital merchandise for the family, as Lily's mother had many local customers in shops and offices around Westmoreland Street, D'Olier Street and the Quays. Here there was always a demand for the earliest British news available — only afterwards would they bother to read the local Dublin papers. The window ledges of the building allowed her to display some of the latest colour magazines and periodicals, while she sold the daily papers from the pram.

This was an important family chore, as the paper stand at the Ballast Office, the headquarters of the Dublin Port and Docks Board, was the only regular source of bread and butter for their tenement home on Marlborough Street. Lily had three older brothers and an ailing father and there was very little money available, as they always seemed to be either in jail, on the run or on strike. Her poor mother was getting beyond carrying heavy loads or walking the streets with papers, or even pushing the old family pram with its big bundles of news from the station.

Lily had left school very early and now, at the age of fifteen, her education depended on her great appetite for reading. Andy, her brother, used to laughingly tell her she was reading all the print of the papers and must have read every book, pamphlet and magazine in God's creation.

There were times when that pram might carry the odd revolver or pistol, hidden for safe keeping under a false bottom after violent city skirmishes. The dilapidated vehicle was, on occasion, brought into active service when sidearms were acquired by Andy or his comrades from inebriated soldiers in the Monto district, or in other public houses on the north side of the inner city. It could then be parked inconspicuously in the back yard of their tenement house, close to the outdoor toilet where the smell was a mortal sin. Apart from earning a small income, the news stand at O'Connell Bridge proved very useful for observing unusual police or military movements in the city, or as a dropping-off point for members of the Dublin Brigade. Lily kept in close contact with Helena Moloney, a friend from the Liberty Hall days, who was based in Westmoreland Street and, with other women in the Co-Op on Eden Quay, was involved in intelligence gathering for the Volunteers.

Lily didn't much mind the early morning run, but she hoped that the railway porter creep with the roving hands wouldn't be around, making her dig for her papers behind the other merchandise while he felt her bottom or groped her breasts with his filthy hands. She was particularly sensitive about her breasts, as she felt they were quite large and not well protected by her light dress, as she did not yet own a protective bra. She was determined to sort him out soon, when the time was right and circumstances would allow, but today acquiring the newspapers for her mother was the critical objective.

As a great fan of Countess Markievicz and a member of the Clan na nGaedheal scouts, she had participated in some training, initially in first aid, physical training and drilling, but had also done some small arms shooting in the foothills of the Dublin mountains with members of Cumann na mBan. She was certainly a young woman of a strong mind, not to be abused by any oul' sleeveen who thought young newspaper sellers could be molested at will.

It was a month or so after the July ceasefire of 1921, and talks were still taking place in London. Lily and most people in Ireland were hoping for a break from the murder and mayhem of the recent months. Her eldest brother, Jim, had arrived in town some days earlier, with a company of sturdy volunteers from the wilds of Wicklow, fully armed and hoping to participate in the displacement of the British military garrison, now mostly confined to barracks. No doubt these British soldiers were hoping to get home soon, for a quieter and safer life than they enjoyed in this country. The armed Volunteers, emboldened by the ceasefire, had also managed to put the skids on some of the more dangerous city-based G-men in the DMP, the Dublin Metropolitan Police, who frequently accompanied the British Army and Black and Tans on raiding parties, or searches for fugitive Volunteers and their supporters.

Her brother Jim had gone to live with their elderly grandparents. And had benefited from the fresh air and decent food, however basic it may have been, down in the mountains around Ballinglen. That area of Wicklow had proved a safe haven for Jim and some others on the run from the British forces. The local Royal Irish Constabulary (RIC) men usually gave the area a wide berth, as they knew how vulnerable and isolated they and their families were in those mountains, with armed volunteers constantly on the lookout. The Volunteers avoided the main roads and made use of some little-known routes to south Wicklow through the Dublin mountains, via Ticknock, Glencullen or Kilmashogue; across the Featherbeds to Glencree and through the Glen of Imaal and onward.

They knew the old route taken across the mountains by the O'Neill and O'Donnell princes of Ulster, who centuries before had escaped from Dublin Castle in the middle of winter to find refuge with the Irish clans who still retained Gaelic dominance in Wicklow. The old mountain trails were later put to good use by Michael Dwyer and his rebel followers during the 1798 period, when they travelled undercover to and from meetings with the United Irishmen and Robert Emmet supporters in Rathfarnham, or even as far away as the Liberties of Dublin.

Lily's father had often told her the story of how the Ulster O'Neills, or 'the Nails,' as they were known, came to be in that part of the country. The escapees from Dublin Castle were rescued and taken in by the O'Byrnes and O'Tooles of Wicklow. Lily had also been well nourished on stories about 1798 and the exploits of Michael Dwyer and his mountain men. She could sing without prompting all the verses of a ballad about his daring escape following a ferocious fight in the Glen of Imaal, which ended with his successful dash to freedom, but the death of his three brave companions.

He baffled his pursuers who followed like the wind,
He swam the River Slaney and left them far behind,
and many a scarlet soldier he promised soon would fall
for those his gallant comrades who died in wild Imaal.

Ticknock, Two Rock Mountain and the hills above Taylor's Grange were previously training grounds for the British Army's 13th Brigade. In recent times, the Fianna Éireann and Clan na nGaedheal had made good use of this rugged area in the foothills of the Dublin mountains, from Taylor's Grange to Kilmashogue and Glencullen; as did the 1st, 2nd, 3rd, and 4th Battalions of the Volunteers. Padraig Pearse, Éamonn Ceannt, Cathal Brugha, Dr Kathleen Lynn and the Countess and their followers knew that area very well indeed from camping, drilling and arms training.

Lily's brother Jim and his comrades kept in close contact with Andy McDonnell, 1st Lieutenant of the local Volunteers, and Jack Courtney and the members of E Company of the Third Battalion, Dublin Brigade, located in the Dublin mountains. In their ranks there were many workers from the granite quarries who could ensure a ready supply of gelignite, detonators and fuses for making grenades and pipe bombs. They had a facility for this work, which was carefully concealed in the Courtney quarry behind Jack Courtney's house up on Kilmashogue mountain. These intimate contacts were to prove vital for their survival and escape when the Civil War erupted in the city and the irregulars had to beat a disorderly retreat back to their secret mountain hideouts, or take refuge in safe houses further south in the middle of the country, or in more isolated places closer to the Wexford border.

Lily hadn't had her full family together since Christmas 1916, after the prisoner releases. She had only been ten years of age at the time. Today she was delighted that Jim, Andy and Jack were still alive and well. Jim, a member of B Company, 3rd Battalion, Dublin Brigade, had continued to be active in Wicklow. She was glad also that they had seen how bad conditions were for her mother and father on Marlborough Street. Andy, a member of the Boland's Mill garrison in 1916, had been on the run for some time and was being actively pursued by the authorities, with the help of a despicable G-man from the Mountjoy Square area, who had known all the lads well since they were teenagers. Only a few weeks earlier, the military had raided Lily's home, wrecking their modest furnishings, forcing her ailing father out of his bed and manhandling her mother when she tried to stop them turning the bed upside down.

To make matters worse, an inebriated neighbour, Maggie Reilly, who had two useless sons in the British Army, was on the footpath calling on the soldiers to 'leave decent loyal people alone and deal with them 'chimney pot fighters' and the 'under the bed fighters' in the basement of the house'. Andy had later paid Mrs Reilly and her husband a late-night visit to remind them in no uncertain terms that her husband or her sons might not survive another finger-wagging performance if it resulted in any serious harm to the O'Neill family.

Lily's brother Jack was the real enigma of the family. He was a natural rebel, but always had a different perspective on the political situation from his brothers. He was a very occasional docker and a more regular drinker, who did spells on the coal boats. He was known to take off unannounced on a tramp ship for a spell; or hop over to see his old friend and relative Whack Reid on the Liverpool docks if the mood took him.

Whack and his brother John Joe, with Lily's brother Andy, were in Boland's Mill during Easter 1916 under Éamon de Valera. Whack had refused to march out of Boland's Mill with de Valera after the surrender at the end of the week's fighting. Under the cover of darkness, he crossed walls and garden fences over the railway line to get to the Liverpool berth on the docks. He sailed that night, asleep in the hold of the ship. He later married in Liverpool and never officially came back to Dublin. He was now working on the Liverpool docks, but kept in frequent contact through unofficial flits on the ferries that regularly crossed the Irish Sea.

Jack was also part of a small socialist group of mainly Citizen Army men and former soldiers who remembered the anti-Larkin activities of some of the more recent 'revolutionaries' in Sinn Féin, who, they argued, had had no qualms about supporting William Martin Murphy and the Dublin Metropolitan Police, the RIC and the British Army against the strikers during the 1913 Lock-Out. His own father, at one time associated with the Invincibles, had not worked since 1913, when he abandoned his dray on O'Connell Bridge and joined the strikers' demonstrating at Nelson's Pillar. He was severely injured in the police baton charge that day and had suffered the effects ever since. Apart from being blacklisted and boycotted by employers, his injuries ensured that he could never again undertake any physical work.

Jack was generally more inspired by the 1917 Russian Revolution than Easter 1916 and he saw himself as more of an internationalist. He encouraged Lily to read everything that James Connolly or Karl Marx wrote and got a regular supply of material from British Labour comrades. He was active in organising the Dublin unemployed to demand that the voice of the poor and underprivileged be heard above the purely nationalistic slogans of the day.

At the time, the trade unions were in retreat, workers' wages were frequently cut and union activists were often victimised. Jack did not hesitate to denounce the deadly use of the British Army, or the Black and Tans, against defenceless people, and he was supportive of those engaged in the struggle for independence. He was a voracious reader and kept Lily busy getting books and socialist literature from England about the international labour movement. In 1930 he actually made his way to Moscow with artist Harry Kernoff, Hannah Sheehy-Skeffington and others in a delegation of Dublin's unemployed.

He was well aware of the ordinary people and was constantly concerned about the large number of maimed and wounded soldiers, some blind and disoriented, on the streets of Dublin. To him, these were the poor unfortunate victims of capitalist wars and human exploitation. He read everything James Connolly wrote and frequently quoted a passage of his, from a little notebook he carried everywhere:

Ireland without its people is nothing to me, and the man who is bubbling over with love and enthusiasm for Ireland can pass unmoved through our streets and witness all the wrong and suffering wrought upon the people of Ireland, aye wrought by Irishmen upon Irishmen and women without burning to end it, is in my opinion a fraud and a liar in his heart.

Today Lily had achieved her primary objective, had secured her parcels of papers, snarled ferociously at the rail porter so that he kept a respectable distance and had run down the commercial delivery slope from the station with her valuable cargo. The wheels of the pram seemed to spin effortlessly now, as she sped towards the Ballast Office with high hopes that the bloodletting of recent years might be over without any loss of life among her poor, beloved family. She knew she might often feel like a young innocent dreamer, but hoped that her heartfelt desire for a glorious Irish Republic might eventually be realised. She knew that her brother Jack's hope for a workers' republic and a fairer and more equal world would be difficult to achieve, but felt it was still a worthy aspiration for him, for her family and, hopefully, for many future Irish generations.

A few weeks later Lily woke with a start in the night to the sound of heavy guns and regular rifle fire. At first it seemed like distant thunder, but she soon realised from the rapidity of the noise that it was heavy guns. She remembered this sound from when the British gunboat *Helga* shelled the city from the Liffey berth at the Custom House Quay in 1916. In those terrible days, her mother and their neighbours in Marlborough Street had to huddle in the basement of their house as chunks of their roof and the top storey smashed to the ground.

She knew now that the city was in a state of war like never before. The repetitive shellfire and crashing masonry of the Four Courts echoed along the banks of the Liffey, informing the citizenry of Dublin that the talking and debating about the Treaty was now over and the bloodletting was back in deadly earnest. This was an outcome she had dreaded for weeks as the opposing sides in the Treaty debate became more and more polarised. The arguments at home and in the city had grown more and more antagonistic, former friends and comrades taking opposing sides and shunning each other on the streets.

Of even greater concern to Lily were the increasingly heated rows among her brothers at home. Jim had aligned with Cathal Brugha and the anti-Treaty republicans, denouncing the proposed Oath of Allegiance to the British Crown as an insult to 'our patriot dead' and the betrayal of our beleaguered comrades in the north. Jack sarcastically asked him had he any idea 'how many bloody Oaths of Allegiance would be required to put a loaf of bread and some butter on a poor man's table?' He was equally dismissive of some emerging Sinn Féin politicians on both sides of the argument who, in his view, 'never gave a damn' for the poor or unemployed of the city. He argued vehemently that it was time the rank and file fighters heeded the advice of James Connolly, who had told the Irish Citizen Army members to hold on to their guns after Easter Week if they managed to survive the Easter Rising.

The final eruption came when Lily's brother Andy arrived home in an army uniform. He had joined the newly formed Free State Army. She knew that Andy believed strongly in Michael Collins and trusted him because of his powerful leadership role in the War of Independence. He admitted that, after serving under him in Boland's Mill during Easter Week, he was not a great fan of de Valera as a soldier. He and others in that garrison felt frustrated by Dev's indecision, as they waited too long behind the walls of the mill while fierce fighting was raging at Clanwilliam House and elsewhere along the Grand Canal close to their position. In fact, Andy often said he was sorry that he didn't refuse to march out for the surrender with Dev; he should instead have slipped over the wall with Whack Reid at the end of the week's fighting.

He had been reassured also, by his friend and comrade Liam Tobin, that Michael Collins saw this deal as a necessary stepping-stone for the eventual realisation of the United Irish Republic that he wanted. He said that no matter what Dev, Brugha or Markievicz believed, the IRA at this time was an under-resourced army, almost a spent force, exhausted and ill-prepared for the continuation of a bloodier struggle against a reinforced British Army. In a personal admission to Lily, he also told her that for the first time in recent years, he would be a paid soldier and he no longer wished to see her, his father and his mother living in such dire poverty.

On 18 January, two days after the Dáil ratified the Treaty and the Provisional Government of the Free State was constituted, a number of men decided to occupy the Rotunda Concert Hall and Pillar Room at the top of O'Connell Street. Among them were Liam O'Flaherty, an ex-British soldier who was editing a paper called *The Workers' Republic* with Roddy Connolly, the son of the executed James Connolly; Jim Phelan, a left-wing member of the IRA; Lily's brother Jack O'Neill from the Dublin Council of the Unemployed and a few hundred supporters. Seán O'Casey regarded Liam O'Flaherty highly as a writer and also agreed with his general political sentiments. These left-wing activists were also aware of other occupations by workers in such places as Limerick and Cork Harbour, and were inspired by the success of the Russian Revolution in 1917. O'Flaherty told the media, 'it was a peaceful protest against the apathy of the authorities in the face of rising unemployment'.

Some members of this group had been holding regular public meetings at Beresford Place on issues such as unemployment, housing, welfare and poverty. They had been gathering increased support among the many unemployed workers, former soldiers and some remnants of the Irish Citizen Army. They were also acting in defiance of the nationalists who they believed had made the Oath of Allegiance their only priority. Given the political leadership of Sinn Féin and the tone of the Treaty debate, they believed that the rights of the ordinary people would likely be completely neglected, and might even be suppressed during the implementation of the proposed 'Free State Treaty'. Their protest was a kind of 'plague on all your bloody works and pomps, what about the poor people?' They had defiantly hung out a red flag over the Rotunda, at the top of O'Connell Street, probably not the wisest thing to do when loyalty to either Green Harp or Red Union Jack were extremely emotive issues at the time.

Lily, along with the men's wives and friends, had gathered bags of bread and fruit from the docks and the market to supply them with some basic provisions for the planned occupation. Bananas and tea were secured on the docks, cabbages in the city markets, bread from a few local bakeries; and a few bottles of porter were gathered from friendly publicans. Supplies, legal or otherwise, were procured in the hope that they could sustain the occupation. It was a peaceful protest, but there were some small arms there, kept for defensive purposes if required.

The occupation met with a lot of hostility, perhaps because of the red flag, as there were already elements in the city totally hostile to anything that smacked of communism. The building was stormed by a large mob, hand-to-hand fighting took place and some shots were fired before a combined force of DMP and Republican Police arrived to restore order. Having held out for four days, the protesters decided to evacuate the Rotunda and quickly dispersed. Liam O'Flaherty and a friend took off for Cork to avoid arrest.

With street fighting raging and the Civil War in full swing, Lily was completely deflated and despondent. She was fearful about the fate of her brothers, who had all stopped coming home to Marlborough Street and were now on opposite sides in the conflict. She wondered why there was so little concern on either side for the thousands of poor people already living in dire straits and now about to be innocent victims of another unforgiving war. The Republican Irregulars had occupied the Ballast Office, making it difficult for Lily or her mother to sell the daily papers.

The recent Government of Ireland Act of 1920 had already split the country and installed an administration in Stormont, while nationalists in the North were being subject to pogroms and violent attacks by sectarian Orange mobs. There appeared to be little consideration for the plight of people in the northern counties as the two new Irish states were born and baptised in blood. She remembered a prophetic passage she had read by James Connolly on the proposed partition of the country, which she had hoped would never come to pass. He predicted that it would unleash 'a carnival of reaction both North and South … would set back the wheels of progress, would destroy the oncoming unity of the Irish labour movement and paralyse all advanced movements while it endured'.

Selling papers on O'Connell Street Bridge had become impossible for some weeks after the fighting started, so Lily reluctantly had to plod her way to a friendly grocer in Townsend Street to get some more credit for essential foodstuffs for home. As she approached her house in Marlborough Street one evening, with a small bag of bread and tea, she was surprised to see one of Mrs Reilly's sons, back from foreign service in the British Army, in a brand-new Free State Army uniform, at the door of their tenement house, smoking a Woodbine. As she passed him at the door, he threw a sarcastic comment over his shoulder at her. 'It's a pity you weren't here earlier Lily, the landlord was here looking for you, he said yer mother hadn't paid him any rent for over a month.'

> But the landlord calls when there's rent to pay,
> The baker sells his bread each day,
> The merchant's coal is burning grey,
> As you sell the morning papers,
> Carrying tales of glorious wars,
> Battles fought for every cause,
> Where the poor do all the dying.
> Oh Lily bright, oh Lily fair,
> though the morning streets are cold and bare,
> warm sunlight will soon fill the air,
> When loved ones are home returning
> Then no more for you a lonely fight,
> Together they will share your strife,
> Where you've kept the home fires burning.'
> ('Lily Bright' was written by the author, c. 2005.)

2

Home Is Where the Heart Is

Tom Geraghty was feeling homesick and generally unhappy with his life when he remembered how long it was since he'd come to work in Manchester. At this stage he had been employed there for over ten years and knew he had no desire to remain in that city for the rest of his life. It had many attractions and life was not particularly unpleasant, but his desire to return home to Dublin was always niggling at him and had grown stronger and more irresistible with each year in that large industrial city.

He had been deported unceremoniously by his father from Dublin to Britain at the tender age of fifteen to prevent him being involved in the War of Independence. His father had succeeded in securing him employment in a large cotton warehousing company. The wages were poor enough and his living accommodation left a lot to be desired.

The Christian Brothers in Dublin's Westland Row School had ensured that Tom was endowed with reasonably good reading and writing skills, useful enough for clerical duties, after years of a tough educational grind under their care. They had also instilled in him deep feelings of national pride and a strong awareness of British injustice during the centuries of their misrule in Ireland.

The nature of the work in Manchester didn't bother him much, but the harsh and unfriendly nature of some of the supervision did. He was often depressed by the dark and dreary conditions of the warehouse in which he worked, the poor wages, his isolated living conditions and the lack of family or friends around him. As a consequence, he had changed jobs a number of times in an effort to improve his lot. He had moved closer to the centre of the city in search of better conditions of employment in unionised firms, as well as greater access to entertainment and social activity. While he had developed some contacts with other young workers in the city, both male and female, he had not formed any bonds of sufficient strength that would encourage him to maintain a permanent presence in England.

During 1918, his father was very unhappy with Tom's involvement in Na Fianna Éireann in Dublin and was determined to prevent him being caught up in physical force activity as hostilities developed in the city. He had therefore brought him to Manchester, without any consultation or forewarning, found him his first job and accommodation in a shoddy lodging house. Then he had left him to make his own way in that strange city. Shortly afterwards, he departed in great haste back to his new family in Dublin. Tom knew that another reason for his exile in Manchester was his father's desire to remove him and his three sisters, Maggie, Lily and Ellie, from the family home to alternative accommodation shortly after their mother died.

His father had remarried and his second wife already had two children, so it was clear that he had concluded that there were too many mouths to feed on his wages, while also maintaining his well-established drinking habit. His decision wasn't all that uncommon in those dark days; when children reached the age of fourteen they were often considered old enough to earn their own living and support themselves outside the family home. Understandably, the unhappy expulsion of the four children would damage relationships in the family for many years and permanently alienated Tom and his sisters from their father.

As a young boy, Tom had joined the Na Fianna Éireann and had narrowly missed out on involvement in the 1916 Rising because of his age – he was only eleven when the fighting broke out. He had been sent home on the Monday morning by the officer in command of his sluagh (company) and told to stay there to mind Fianna camping equipment and billy cans until the fighting was over. The family was living in Clare Lane at that time, close to the rear entrance of Trinity College. During the week's fighting Tom was upset by the subservient welcome given to the British Army by many students of the college. He was particularly infuriated when he saw Trinity College students actually digging up cobblestone streets to facilitate the British military digging in with their heavy guns. While the fighting raged around the city, he tried to keep up his lagging spirits by singing the Fianna Éireann anthem to himself:

Hark to the tramp of the young guard of Éireann,
Firm is each footstep and erect is each head,
Soldiers of freedom, un-fearing and eager
To follow the teachings of our heroes dead.
On for freedom na Fianna Éireann,
Set we our faces to the dawning day,
The day in our own land when strength and daring
Shall end for ever more the Saxon sway.

He did keep himself busy that week bringing feed and water to the horses trapped in stables close to his home. That involved the risky business of climbing over walls and gates carrying buckets of water and bags of fodder. The heavy fighting had seriously disrupted all movement on the streets and prevented the regular horse carters and cabbies from visiting the stables to service their horses.

Tom loved the horses and knew they were suffering from neglect during that week. He was proud of a small job he had delivering groceries and other essentials to the well-appointed houses on Merrion Square with a pony and trap owned by a local shop. The small earnings from this activity helped bolster his mother's meagre income, and gave him enough to keep a small amount for books, comics and toffees. His love of horses and knowledge of the city streets would prove invaluable years later when he secured a full-time job with responsibility for transporting heavy hardware materials from the Dublin docks and warehouses up to the Huggard Stores in the Liberties.

Life in the 'hungry twenties' was difficult and lonely for a young emigrant in a foreign city. Because of his size friends called him 'Little

Tommy'. He knew very little about Manchester before he arrived there, but remembered well a song he had heard sung at a Fianna camp about the execution of the Manchester Martyrs – Allen, Larkin and O'Brien. These Fenians were executed in November 1867 following an abortive attack on a prison van escorting Fenian prisoners named Kelly and Deasy, which resulted in the death of a prison guard. The words of that song raised his hopes that there were likely to be other Irish people in the city who shared his own Fenian sentiments:

Attend you gallant Irishmen and listen for a while,
I'll sing to you the praises of the sons of Erin's Isle,
It's of those gallant heroes who voluntarily ran
To release two Fenian prisoners from an English prison van
…

The story continues with the full details of the escapade, and concludes with the often-used patriotic ballad sentiment:

So now kind friends I will conclude, I think it would be right,
That all true-hearted Irishmen together should unite,
Together should sympathise, my friends, and do the best you can,
To keep the memory evergreen, of the boys that smashed the van.

As a young Irish emigrant, Tom was sometimes subjected to an element of ignorant hostility in the workplace from older Empire loyalist types, or from former soldiers. One individual frequently spoke sneeringly about the treachery of the 'Sinn Féiners in Ireland, stabbing decent English people in the back during their terrible war.' One particularly unpleasant foreman insisted on calling him 'Little Paddy' and regularly sought to make fun of his strong Dublin accent. Although on occasion his blood would be boiling, he had acquired a strict discipline of keeping tight control on his temper in the workplace. Privately, he felt he had succeeded in achieving the perfect retaliation when he was able to participate in undercover fund-raising for the 'dreaded Sinn

Féiners'. He was particularly pleased when he learned of the escape of a few prominent Sinn Féin prisoners from Strangeways Gaol in Manchester in October 1919, obviously with local assistance. After that news, he was determined to seek out these local volunteers and offer his services.

He made early contact with fellow republicans at a Manchester Martyrs commemoration event and began to work closely with an organiser in the city named McGrath. His new comrades advised him, where possible, to avoid the normal social clubs or pubs associated with gatherings of Irish people. They were well aware that the police in Manchester were always on the lookout for supporters of the Irish republican cause. Tom was not a regular drinker, so he accepted their advice readily, although he did at times regret that he could not have greater social contact with more of his fellow Irish people in the city.

The most practical alternative for him was to frequent socialist, labour and trades union venues, where he met many interesting English, Welsh and Scottish people and learned a lot more about politics from them. They tended to focus their attention more on the difficult working conditions at the time, the low rates of pay, the issues of welfare and unemployment. He found they also had a much broader view of how the world was organised in favour of the rich and powerful people in both Britain and Ireland. Their general approach to human rights made a lot of sense to him. The labour-minded people he met, some of whom were second- or third-generation Irish or Scottish, were generally more sympathetic to the Irish cause. None of them ever made fun of his name or nationality. As a consequence, he regularly attended meetings, lectures and evening classes organised by the trade unions, the Trades Council or the local co-ops.

Apart from their general educational value, these engagements strengthened Tom's belief in the need for a much stronger socialist labour movement in Ireland, one that could cross all national boundaries and prejudices, upholding human rights for all, irrespective of nationality or religion. He felt these fellow workers in Manchester were much closer to him and to the values of Jim Larkin, James Connolly, Countess Markievicz and the Irish Citizen Army than were

Arthur Griffith, William Cosgrave, John Redmond, Kevin O'Higgins or any of the current Free Staters or masters of Cumann na nGaedheal.

He often wondered how, between 1921 and 1931, the abolition of poverty never got the same attention at home as the abolition of the British Oath of Allegiance had and continued to have, even after such a devastating civil war. He kept in close contact with home by reading every Irish newspaper he could find and also by keeping up a regular correspondence with his elder sister Maggie.

As the twenties wore on, he became aware of a growing change of political sentiment in Ireland, which he hoped would bring better times for the Irish people. During those years, Tom was very well aware of acute poverty, hardship and emigration at home and a growing national support for those who had opposed the 1921 Treaty. He knew that in recent years many disillusioned republicans had emigrated to the United States and Canada, of absolute necessity, with many more even travelling as far afield as Australia in search of work.

That was also obvious in Britain, where many new Irish arrivals flocked every day to the cities of Manchester, Liverpool, Birmingham and London. Tom recognised that many workers from Mayo, Donegal and other western counties, who had spent time working on farms in Scotland or the Northern shires of Britain, were now flooding into the British cities for better-paid industrial or construction work.

While Tom retained a strong personal attachment to the concept of a United Ireland, he was increasingly concerned that the 1921 Treaty, the brutal Civil War that followed, and the imposition of partition on the country had resulted in creating two backward states in Ireland, both defined more by religious prejudice and intolerance than by any genuine concern for people, be they Catholic, Protestant or Dissenter. The curious aspect of this for him, in Manchester, was that wherever emigrants came from, North or South, they were all seen as the same 'Irish emigrants', although there was growing evidence of a stronger Orange presence in some parts of the city.

In 1925 he had read the powerful words of W.B. Yeats, by then a Senator in the Free State Senate, who had warned the establishment, during a debate on legislation for the prohibition of divorce, which a minority of the people considered grossly oppressive, that if the Free

State was 'governed by Catholic ideas and by Catholic ideas alone you will never get the North'. Yeats then reminded them about the major historic contribution of Protestants to the cause of Ireland:

I am proud to consider myself a typical man of that minority. We against whom you have done this thing, are no petty people. We are one of the great stocks of Europe. We are the people of Burke; we are the people of Grattan; we are the people of Swift, the people of Emmet, the people of Parnell. We have created most of the modern literature of this country. We have created the best of its political intelligence.

During the 1920s, religious intolerance was even worse in Northern Ireland than it was in the South. From the foundation of the Northern Ireland entity, there were regular outbreaks of religious bigotry and violent pogroms against Catholics. Many of these attacks were condoned openly by Unionist politicians and the Orange Order, which maintained a very powerful presence. Attacks frequently extended to major places of work or to local communities, resulting in serious segregation. The trade unions and some clergy sought to mitigate the hostilities, but a lot of the loyalist activity was intended to keep their Catholic neighbours, who were considered enemies of the state, in their proper subservient place. This part of Great Britain was clearly constructed as a 'Protestant state for a Protestant people' with British politicians largely unconcerned about the treatment being doled out to the Catholic minority living under the writ of the Crown.

In June 1929, James Geoghegan of Fianna Fáil won the first by-election for Dev's new party, securing a win in Longford-Westmeath and sending shock waves through the Cumann na nGaedheal establishment. The result heralded the possibility that following a general election, Fianna Fáil could conceivably lead the next government.

Dev's relegation of the British Oath of Allegiance to the status of 'an empty formula' had somehow transformed the political landscape. Now anti-Treaty TDs could hope to lead a majority in Dáil Éireann, with the support of the Labour Party. While Sinn Féin and Labour were in some internal disarray, Tom was certain that the general mood of the Irish people was leaning more towards Fianna Fáil.

While this may not have been universal love, or even wholehearted endorsement, of Dev or his party, it was a recognition that Fianna Fáil offered the most likely prospect for fundamental change. Even committed supporters of Sinn Féin and the Labour Party were beginning to realise that Fianna Fáil was the most likely party to change the balance of power in Dáil Éireann and enable the country to move forward. The wounds of the recent conflicts were deep and memories strong, but Tom hoped that this political shift could herald a new beginning for the country. He regretted that in effect it might mean that again 'Labour Must Wait', but for many good reasons, he thought it was time for a new government.

This development was all the prompting Tom needed to raid his hard-earned savings in the British Post Office and head back home to Dublin. He was unsure how he would find his lost city after all these years, but was elated by the prospect of seeing his sisters again, meeting old friends and enjoying a leisurely stroll along the granite banks of the Liffey.

He had longed for many years to climb the Wicklow mountains again, to see the sun rise over Dublin Bay, or breathe in the sweet fresh air of spring while camping on Kilmashogue mountain. His sister Maggie had promised him that he could stay with her and Ellie while he found a suitable place for himself. He wondered now why he had not taken the decision to go home many years earlier.

When he arrived in Dublin, Tom was elated to be home at last. He was surprised by how much his mood was lifted by the change of accents, the familiar facial features of passers-by, the cries of newspaper sellers, the sound of street singers, the clatter of horse-drawn vehicles, the willingness of people to chat, the streets full of memories and the general friendly character of the city of Dublin.

He was home at last, after a long and difficult journey, and was determined to make the most of his homecoming. The one dark shadow clouding his blue sky and tempering the warm sunshine of his disposition was the absence of many people he once knew and loved.

Some were dead, some had emigrated and many others were shattered and unable to come to terms with their broken dreams.

A lot had changed during his absence. The Civil War had divided the whole country. The savagery of the conflict and the executions and murder of so many good people had left a bitter legacy for many families. The years that followed the conflict had seen cuts in pensions, wages and social benefits, along with increased unemployment and emigration. Teachers and civil servants had all taken pay reductions; and pay rates in most of the private sector were generally poor.

Big Jim Larkin, the great hope of the Irish labour movement, had come home in 1923, after his release from imprisonment in Sing Sing for anti-war activities in the USA. He had left Ireland for the United States in 1914, a short time after the 1913 Lock-Out. On his return in 1923 he had become embroiled in a very divisive internal dispute with the leadership of his own Irish Transport and General Workers' Union (ITGWU). In the early twenties the Irish trade union movement was already highly fragmented with a large number of small competing unions, some newly Irish-based unions and others part of older British unions.

The feud between William O'Brien and Larkin, in the largest union in the country – it had over 100,000 members – had been an unfortunate conflict between old friends and comrades and became extremely destructive. The marked difference between Larkin, the revolutionary, with his 'Divine Gospel of Discontent' and O'Brien, essentially a social reformer, was evident. But this dispute proved to be less about revolution and reform than about political passion and personal power. Their personalities were obviously totally incompatible as leaders of the same trade union organisation. The likelihood of a revolution was very slim after the Civil War, so the man who controlled the organisation won the dispute. Larkin was dismissed from his own union and the whole sorry affair ended up in a bitter court case. The conflict severely weakened the influence of the Irish labour movement as a whole at a time when it was most needed. By the end of the decade the ITGWU's membership had dropped from 100,000 to a mere 16,000.

Jim Larkin was now leading a new trade union, the Workers' Union of Ireland (WUI), which had been formed by his brother Peter Larkin. After the deaths of James Connolly and Michael Mallin in 1916, and Liam Mellows in 1922, the formal leadership of the labour movement was in the hands of William O'Brien of the ITGWU and Tom Johnson, leader of the Labour Party, which at that time was part of the union organisation. The O'Brien–Larkin split of 1923 was to haunt the trade union movement for decades and seriously damaged the ability of the Labour Party to develop itself as a serious alternative to the pro- and anti-Treaty parties that had essentially evolved from the Sinn Féin movement. This division was not healed until 1959, when the united Irish Congress of Trade Unions was formed, with most trade unions participating.

Although the Labour Party had accepted the Treaty and was opposed to the Civil War, there was no new dawn for the labour movement in the new Free State. This was evident in the new Dáil, when the Labour Party sought to amend the draft Constitution by including part of the very progressive 1919 Democratic Programme, the Minister of Home Affairs, Kevin O'Higgins, dismissed the proposed amendment as 'largely poetry' and declared it would be unwise to include in the Constitution 'what certainly looks like a Communist doctrine'.

Tom Johnson realised also that the abstention policy of Sinn Féin and later, for a while, Fianna Fáil, was a major obstacle to any progress on social issues. Labour was opposed to the Oath of Allegiance, but believed it could be removed from within the Dáil rather than from outside. In January 1925, Johnson wrote an open letter to de Valera in which he publicly criticised the policy of abstention, pointing out that the failure of republicans to recognise the Constitution 'would destroy all hope of social change in this generation'. This probably had some influence on de Valera's thinking – as he eventually brought Fianna Fáil into the Dáil and described the Oath of Allegiance as an 'empty formula'.

From the day he arrived back in Dublin Tom made it a priority to find a regular job that would enable him to remain there. He had acquired significant skills in warehousing and shipping procedures, which made him quite a valuable employee for any business involved in import or export activities. He emphasised this in his many job applications and hoped for the best. For some months he survived by doing a variety of odd handyman jobs in carpentry and home repair, or improvement work for individuals, using skills he had largely inherited from his father.

Eventually he landed his ideal job as a general warehouse storeman in a company called James Huggard and Sons Ltd, which was based in Cornmarket in the Liberties of Dublin city. The Huggard family were northern Protestants who owned a hardware business, with a number of import franchises, and a company called Irish Coppersmiths, which distributed and repaired copper boilers and other copper products. The coppersmith business was based close to the company's Cornmarket premises in Lamb Alley, facing the remnants of Dublin's old city wall.

His job was at a small hardware firm, virtually a two-person operation, with himself as storeman and one female clerical employee responsible for the office, telephones, post and accounts. His stores duties ranged from importing, storing, sorting and dispatching, loading, and anything else required to keep the business turning over. Curiously enough, although his employer was a supporter of the Orange Order, on a personal level Tom found he was a very reasonable person to work for.

An important benefit of his new job was the availability of accommodation over the stores, which provided Tom with a much-wanted home and his employer with a ready-made caretaker for his premises. He was to work with the Huggard Company for more than twenty-three years.

3

Church and State in Close Embrace

In the early 1930s Ireland had many economic, social and political issues to contend with. The country had its own particular home-grown issues, but it was also not immune to the impact of the global economic crisis that had hit most developed countries. The USA was struggling with the consequences of the great crash of 1929; unemployment was close to three million in Britain and had reached six million in Germany.

Irish farmers were in deep arrears as a result of land annuity payments, a feudal hangover from British rule, which was being vigorously disputed in most rural areas. There was little protection for either Irish industry or agriculture. Irish products in the home market had to compete with imports from the rest of the world. As a direct consequence, there was a lot of distress and dissatisfaction in the country, which was directed at the Cosgrave government.

Ten years after the 1921 Treaty many people had concluded that the government had become too close to Britain to take the radical steps necessary to assert the true interests of the Irish people. The climate was ripe for change across the globe, not all of which was to prove beneficial for humanity over the coming decades. Fascism was already politically established in Italy and its seeds had been firmly sown in

Germany and Spain, while the fear of communism had been stoked to a level of hysteria in some quarters, including Ireland.

Many Catholic bishops and clergy in Ireland welcomed the strident anti-communist activities of the fascists. This was clearly demonstrated later by their public support for General Franco's military attack on the legitimately elected Republican Government of Spain. Apparently, in the early thirties, they could readily 'discern' dangerous communistic tendencies in Fianna Fáil, Labour and Sinn Féin, although Dev himself appeared to be too pious to be easily painted as a red.

In the general election of February 1932, Fianna Fáil emerged with 72 TDs versus 57 for Cumann na nGaedheal, while Labour secured seven, with two Independent Labour and 15 independent and farmer representatives. Thomas J. O'Connell, the leader of the Labour Party, lost his seat in Mayo to a Fianna Fáil candidate.

Prior to the election there had been an increase in IRA activity. The government, with Eoin O'Duffy as Garda Commissioner, responded with the Public Safety Act 1931. This draconian act empowered the authorities to arrest, detain and try suspects before military tribunals and carry out executions without the normal rules of evidence or defence. There was some limited activity by the IRA, but, more important, there was a strong reaction by the clergy to the policy proposals of Saor Éire, a socialist republican party associated with the IRA, whose members were determined to continue a physical force campaign for a united Ireland. However, Saor Éire never succeeded in gaining any significant support either inside or outside the IRA.

In October 1931 the Catholic hierarchy issued a statement enflaming public alarm about the imminent threat of revolution and communism:

> *We cannot remain silent in the face of the growing evidence of a campaign of revolution and communism, which if allowed to run its course unchecked, must end in the ruin of Ireland, both soul and body ... We appeal most earnestly with deepest anxiety to all our people and especially the young ... Surely the ranks of the communist revolution are no place for an Irish boy of Catholic instincts.*

As a consequence, many republican and labour activists came to describe the days of 1931 and early 1932 as equal to the worst days of terror in 1922–23. The bishops and the government had initiated a 'Red Scare', uncovering active communists in virtually every town and village in the country. Many social activists or republicans were jailed by the military tribunals, as the police found vast numbers of 'communist conspirators' that the tiny Irish Communist Party of that time never knew they had.

Most of the illegal activity in the country actually arose from land disputes and hard-pressed farmers withholding unpopular land annuity payments, which they could not pay. Some were charged with resisting the bailiffs who were trying to collect the payments, often with the support of local IRA units.

Peadar O'Donnell, the Donegal editor of the republican paper *An Phoblacht*, was a firm advocate of strong social action by the IRA rather than a futile return to the gun. He viewed the land annuities as a major injustice, imposed during British rule, which should be abolished by any government of an independent Ireland. He advocated withholding annuity payments as a legitimate act of civil disobedience, in prefer-ence to a continuation of physical force activities by republicans.

Sinn Féin also wanted the general election to achieve a Fianna Fáil victory for a 'Dev In and Prisoners Out' result. With the support of Labour, de Valera did immediately set about fulfilling his election promise of removing the Oath of Allegiance, which turned out to be more difficult than he expected because of the opposition of the Seanad and vigorous external challenges from the British government. The British argued that this change would mean a complete repu-diation of the Treaty of 1921, something that was not being sought. However, de Valera was determined to get rid of the Oath and believed that the majority in the country now supported him in that policy.

In a surprise move towards the end of 1932, de Valera, sensing the mood of the country, called a snap general election for January 1933. The result of that election increased the number of Fianna Fáil TDs to 77 and Labour TDs to eight. Cumann na nGaedheal dropped to 48 seats, a loss of nine TDs. The Centre Party, which had incorporated the Farmers' Party, secured 11 TDs.

Labour loyally supported the new Fianna Fáil government, as an independent political party, but did not itself enter government. With this impressive win behind him, de Valera removed General Eoin O'Duffy as Commissioner of the Garda Síochána and released hundreds of political prisoners. It was estimated, at the time, that there were as many as 50,000 members of the IRA in the country. Apart from marching and drilling in fields, they were involved in very little political activity, but did generally support Fianna Fáil in the election. Their lack of political engagement in the state was to change dramatically with the rise of the 'Blueshirts' under Eoin O'Duffy.

There was also a tiny Communist Party with branches in Dublin and Belfast but with a very small membership. The Dublin party was so small that they were set up in secrecy in a small room rented in 5 Leinster Street, to the subsequent consternation of the landlady, when she learned who the renters were.

Lily O'Neill and her brother Jack were regularly among those who attended political gatherings in Connolly House in Great Strand Street, or in the Workers' College on Eccles Street, the home of Mrs Despard. A range of classes and discussions took place in these venues, and speakers included Frank Ryan, Peadar O'Donnell, Mrs Despard, young Jim Larkin, Roddy Connolly, Mary MacSwiney, Maude Gonne, George Gilmore, Louie Bennett, Brian O'Neill, Hanna Sheehy-Skeffington. These invited speakers would often be asked to talk, lead discussions or answer questions on topical economic or political issues affecting workers and the community at large.

One regular attendee at these sessions was Tom Geraghty, who had recently returned from Britain. Tom was surprised to learn through a casual conversation that Lily O'Neill, a young Communist Party member, was originally from a place called Asylum Yard. This was the location of a few small sub-standard cottages, off Townsend Street in the City Quay area, near the Dublin docks. Curiously enough, this was where his own family home had been at the time of his birth and where he had spent his earliest childhood years. That was just a few years before Lily was born. His family had later moved on to Clare Lane and had little memory of the O'Neills as family neighbours.

From then on, Tom was more interested in Lily than in any of the eminent guest speakers. He was particularly attracted by her lively spirit, self-assuredness, strong opinions and ability to challenge, irrespective of how eminent the speaker might be. He had a good laugh on one occasion when Lily and Peadar O'Donnell were having a disagreement and Peadar joked, 'Sure, anyway, the O'Neills and O'Donnells were always at loggerheads!'

These peaceful political and educational activities were to be violently curtailed in the early thirties; Connolly House, in Great Strand Street, was regularly besieged by mobs of protesters. In 1933, crowds gathered outside the building at night and tried to break in or set fire to the building. These assaults culminated in March 1935 with an attack by street gangs, encouraged by members of the clergy, that was so violent that the defenders had to escape for their lives across the roofs of adjacent buildings. A few shots were fired by a number of the defenders, with handguns, to try to discourage the attackers, but they were eventually overwhelmed by the sheer size and ferocity of the mob outside. On that particular occasion, it was clear that the attackers wanted to put a stop to all meetings and classes in this 'dangerous left-wing venue'. They were absolutely determined to burn the building down, irrespective of who was inside.

Fires were lit with stolen furniture from a factory next door and lighted material was pushed through the letterbox. There was very little effort by the police to curtail the activity of the mob; according to one participant they were 'more concerned with the continuous movement of traffic on Capel Street and Swift's Row than dispersing the law-breakers'. This time the small number of defenders inside the building could not withstand the attack and the angry protesters proceeded to burn down the building. The fire not only destroying a building, but effectively seeking to eradicate completely the legacy of Connolly and Larkin, Michael Mallon, Rosie Hackett, Helena Moloney, James Fintan Lalor, Michael Davitt, Mary MacSwiney and many more radical patriots.

Also burned at the stake of history were the hopes and aspirations of the members of the Irish Citizen Army, of the working class and of small farmer volunteers, who had given so much to establish a more equal and more tolerant society in Ireland. While their ideas could not be placed before a military firing squad, the space to express and develop ideas in their capital city could be eradicated by means of arson at the hands of a sectarian mob.

The political and educational activities of Tom and Lily were immediately curtailed then and they became further restricted when they decided to get married and start their own family. They made their home in Cornmarket, in rooms owned by Tom's employer, above the stores where he worked.

Although the public meetings and lectures were now finished, they had succeeded in establishing a small oasis for free thinking and debate, where family and friends could gather in their home at the very heart of the 'rebel Liberties'. In that intimate setting, over many a cup of tea and a rare bottle of stout, serious events in recent history were remembered, discussed, and dissected by close friends. There were many heated arguments and disagreements about the recent past, but in general there was a consensus of disappointment about the kind of country that all those years of fighting, human sacrifice and suffering had produced for the ordinary people.

One of the issues often hotly discussed was the impact of an Irish form of 'social puritanism' that had been imposed on the people by the Free State establishment during the late twenties and early thirties and had, unfortunately, continued under de Valera's government. It was argued that the Church and State leaders of the time were obsessed by the threat of international communism and had such an excessive concern about the sexual behaviour of the people that they neglected many of the most pressing problems really facing them. That concern about sexual matters and the view that there was a need for legislation to combat a decline in moral standards gave rise to the establishment of the little-remembered, but significant in its impact, Carrigan Committee. This committee, chaired by William Carrigan KC, met in 1929–30 during General Eoin O'Duffy's reign as Commissioner of the Garda Síochána.

It could be argued that this committee was required to review and update the older Criminal Law of 1880/1885 and in response to worrying Garda statistics relating to violence against women – issues relating to prostitution, unmarried mothers, sexual attacks on minors and such matters. What was not envisaged was a complete review of our morality, permissive behaviour, social affairs, entertainment, dancing, homosexuality, incest, policing and contraception, all without any essential information or public debate, even in the Dáil.

Ireland by this stage could be described as a relatively stable and largely peaceful country with a restored legal system largely in line with the previous British system. It might have been timely to review older legislation from the British era, but to make sweeping changes in so many sensitive areas, without public discourse, would seem somewhat excessive in a democracy.

In 1924, the Free State Government had turned its back on the largely successful and popular Sinn Féin Courts system and had restored the legal status quo in line with the original British system. Curiously enough, the Sinn Féin Courts, under the presidency of James Creed Meredith KC, a Protestant who later became a Quaker, had attracted much praise; for example, Hugh Martin, Irish correspondent of the *Daily News*, wrote: 'Ireland is taking pleasure in Law and Order for the first time within the memory of man.' Incidentally, Meredith was the grandfather of Des's partner, Rosheen, who is the only child of his daughter Brenda. His other daughter, Moira, had three children; the only one still surviving is the well-known sculptor Rowan Gillespie.

Other praise for Meredith came from a landlord, Lord Monteagle, who pointed out that 'The Sinn Féin Courts are steadily extending their jurisdiction and dispensing justice even-handedly between man and man, Catholic and Protestant, farmer and shopkeeper, grazier and cattle driver, landlord and tenant.' It might also be remembered that Meredith had a high regard for the ancient Irish legal system and the Brehon Laws, which considered trees to be so important that their protection was regulated strictly in law. In fact, Meredith was the last judge in Ireland to make a ruling under Brehon Law – he ruled that a father should pay maintenance in respect of his child, even though the child had been born out of wedlock.

There was considerable evidence in the early thirties that the State was extremely cautious about changing any laws without seeking direction from the bishops of the Catholic Church. O'Duffy, during his period of office, had also ensured that An Garda Síochána had adopted a broadly Catholic moral code and he had reinforced that, as reported in the *Garda Review*, by facilitating large Garda pilgrimages to Rome in 1928 and to Lourdes in 1930.

Apart from a normal judicial review being undertaken by the government, a wider concern was expressed by the Catholic bishops; there was, they claimed, an urgent need to regulate sexual behaviour because of an increasing 'looseness of morals' in the State. Clerics regularly expressed the view that unregulated cinemas and dance halls were 'schools of scandal'; they railed against the 'misuse of motor cars for sexual purposes' and against 'late-night dancing'; and expressed a general hostility to 'popular amusements being carried on in the absence of supervision'. Seán O'Casey was to write sarcastically in his autobiography:

> *The orders will be let loose over the country to tighten up the faith of the people, the Civil Service will become the Third Order of Saint Formulas, the Knights of Columbanus will become the soldiers of the legion of the prayer guard, the Pope's brass band will be developed into a symphony orchestra, Armagh conducting with Dublin playing first fiddle; the gay rustle of a girl's skirt will be hushed by the discreet rustle of a priest's cassock and the friar's gown, the priests will drag the people of Ireland into heaven by the scruff of their necks.*

In 1934, Ireland hosted the great Eucharistic Congress, which brought thousands of bishops and clerics from many distant lands to celebrate our country's fidelity to the Roman Catholic faith. They were determined to ensure that a Catholic Ireland 'can take its place among the nations of the earth' – not quite as Robert Emmet, a Protestant republican, might have envisaged Ireland in his speech from the dock before his execution. Our great historic achievement was to have consolidated two confessional states in Ireland, one for Protestants and another for Catholics. The Dissenters, of all persuasions, could henceforth keep their mouths shut, or emigrate.

The Carrigan Committee never published a report and its findings were entrusted to a secretive Dáil committee, which also failed to publish a public report. There appeared to be a view by the government and among the bishops that the conclusions of these bodies might be a cause for scandal among an uninformed public. They might serve to undermine the belief that the social order in Ireland was somehow superior to that existing in other less religious jurisdictions.

While the Department of Justice, for good technical reasons, was scathing in its criticisms of the recommendations of the Carrigan Committee, it fell to the Fianna Fáil Minister for Justice James Geoghegan TD to introduce the Criminal Law Amendment Act 1935 and an associated piece of legislation, the Public Dance Halls Act 1935.

Among the multiplicity of issues, not properly debated, dealt with under these Acts were a ban on contraceptives, soliciting, brothel-keeping and prostitution; an age of consent for carnal knowledge and sexual intercourse; and regulations relating to unmarried mothers and their offspring, sexual diseases, treatment of offenders and homosexuality. In addition, the regulation and control of dance halls and entertainment venues was introduced. In line with the law of unintended consequences, many of the best communal features of rural Ireland, such as house dances, crossroads dancing, set dances, wakes, weddings and traditional music sessions, fell victim to this overwhelmingly authoritarian set of regulations.

With one mighty sweep, these laws were intended to make Ireland a safer, more virtuous and holier place for people to dwell in, before all the comely maidens and the virtuous men would eventually ascend happily to heaven. The State's many responses to these complex and diverse issues and the accepted policy by many subsequent governments, of outsourcing the enforcement and supervision of such delicate matters to religious orders and other unregulated Church bodies, has proved to be one of the most undesirable and seriously mistaken policies, for the unfortunate people affected by them, since the foundation of this State.

Many decent Catholic nuns and priests, and those of other denominations, have always made a huge contribution to Irish society, motivated by their Christian values and commitment to people's welfare. Unfortunately, however, the abuse of power and privilege and intervention into the political realm by some Princes of the Church and their institutions has often betrayed the wonderful work of these great people.

In the North, in April 1934, James Craig (Lord Craigavon) and the Orange Order were consolidating their sectarian grip on Northern Ireland. Speaking in Stormont, Craig 'could not but have been delighted with the sectarian consolidation of the Irish Two-State Solution':

> *I have always said that I am an Orangeman first and a politician and a member of this Parliament afterwards ... in the South they boasted of a Catholic State. They still boast of Southern Ireland being a Catholic State. All I boast of is that we are a Protestant Parliament and a Protestant State.*

The Minister for Labour in the North, J.M. Andrews, speaking at an Orange Order demonstration in July 1933, said:

> *Another allegation made against the Government, which is untrue, is that 31 porters at Stormont are Roman Catholic. I have investigated the matter and I have found that there are 30 Protestants and only one Roman Catholic there, only temporarily.*

Basil Brooke, a member of the Northern Ireland Government, speaking to the Derry Unionist Association in 1934, could unashamedly say: 'I recommend those people who are loyalists not to employ Roman Catholics, 99 per cent of whom are disloyal.' This pattern of sectarian discrimination was encouraged by Unionist politicians across the province.

In Mayo, in January 1931, the library committee of the County Council refused to appoint Ms Dunbar Harrison, a Protestant, to the position of librarian. The Catholic Dean of Tuam, Monsignor E.A. D'Alton, supported this decision:

[W]e are not appointing a washerwoman or a mechanic, but an educated girl who ought to know what books to put into the hands of Catholic boys and girls of this country ... is it safe to entrust a girl who is not a Catholic, and is not in sympathy with Catholic views, with their handling?

Speaking in the Dáil on the same subject, de Valera said:

If it is a mere passive position of handing down books that are asked for, then the librarian has no particular duty for which religion should be regarded as a qualification, but if ... it is active work of a propagandist educational character - I believe it to be such if it is to be of any value at all and worth the money spent on it - then I say the people of Mayo, a county where, I think - I forget the figures - over 98 per cent of the population is Catholic, are justified in insisting upon a Catholic librarian.

4

Tryin' to Die for Ireland

*In Bodenstown churchyard there lies a green grave
and wildly around it let the winter winds wave
Small shelter I ween are the ruined walls there
When the storm sweeps down o'er the plains of Kildare.
Once I lay on that sod it lies over Wolfe Tone
and thought how he perished in prison alone
his friends unavenged his country unfree
how bitter I thought was the patriot's mead.*
(Traditional republican song – author unknown)

Generations of Irish republicans, seeking to reaffirm their desire to uphold the traditional values of the United Irishmen, have for many years made an annual pilgrimage to the grave of Wolfe Tone in Bodenstown, County Kildare. This event has survived over more than two centuries as a form of spiritual renewal of the people's vows of fidelity to the republican ideal. Various shades of republicans have taken the time to gather at this peaceful location to reaffirm their dedication to the glorious aspirations of liberty, equality and fraternity, the *liberté, égalité et fraternité* of the French Revolutionaries of 1789 and the United Irishmen of 1798.

These were the anti-sectarian principles espoused by Tone and his followers as the guiding principles for their desire to unite the people of Ireland: 'Break the Connection with England'. They hoped to overcome the 'Catholic, Protestant and Dissenter' labels, establish the common name of Irishman and Irishwoman and to replace the British monarchy with a republican form of government. This was also the path followed by Robert Emmet and his followers in 1803; and it has remained the aspiration of Young Irelanders, Fenians, Land Leaguers, Volunteers, the Citizen Army, Sinn Féin and many more ever since.

In O'Casey's classic play *The Plough and the Stars*, the hilarious exchange between the young Mrs Gogan, Fluter Good and Uncle Peter illustrates the status that the annual visit to Bodenstown had, at least in one Dublin tenement house. Mrs Gogan, admiring Uncle Peter's elaborate and colourful uniform of the Irish National Foresters for the march at Bodenstown, remarks,

The foresthers' is a gorgeous dhress, when yous are goin' along an I see them wavin an' noddin an waggin', ... tryin' to die for Ireland!

Peter: There's not many that's talking can say that for twenty-five years he never missed a pilgrimage to Bodenstown!

Fluter: You're always blowin' about going to Bodenstown. D'ye ever think no one but yourself ever went to Bodenstown?

Peter: I'm not blowin' about it; but there's not a year that I go there but I pluck a leaf off Tone's grave, an' this very day me prayer book is nearly full of them.

Fluter: Then Fluter has a visa-versa opinion of them that put ivy leaves into their prayer books, scabbin it on the clergy, an tryin to out-do th'haloes o'th saints, be lookin as if he was wearin around his head a glittherin aroree boree allis! Sure, I don't care a damn if you slept in Bodenstown! You can take your breakfast, dinner, an tea on th' grave in Bodenstown, if ye like ... for Fluter.

The religiosity and humour of the exchange captures very well the reverence associated with the annual pilgrimage. Curiously enough, while many visitors to that grave would remember the 1798 exploits of the Catholic Father Murphy and the Wexford United Irishmen, far fewer would remember the sacrifices and exploits of the mainly Protestant or Presbyterian rebels in Ulster or the other Protestant comrades and the United Irishmen Protestant weavers in the Liberties of Dublin. Neither would Uncle Peter see any irony in the fact that plucking ivy leaves was done to remember Parnell, another sad victim of Ireland's religious fundamentalism. Nor would the frequent recital of a decade of the Rosary at the conclusion of the political speeches have given Uncle Peter a second thought, proudly decked out in his green-wagging forester's plumage.

Lily and Tom rarely failed to attend the annual Bodenstown commemoration, which was for them as much a family gathering as a political event. It was an ideal place for old friends and comrades to seek each other out and keep up with the latest news and gossip. The responsibility for the official event usually lay with the National Graves Association, so access to the grave was carefully protected by one of their 'true and trusted' from year to year.

However, the local village of Sallins – and, after the event, Clane or Prosperous – became the unofficial centres for great celebration and jollification on the day and frequently into the night. The Fianna Éireann contingents would camp along the canal bank and in the surrounding fields close to Sallins, as would the Clan na nGaedheal Girl Scouts with Cumann na mBan and other family campers. Some contingents from distant parts would sleep rough or in caravans and tents, or in battered old buses or lorries hired or borrowed for the occasion.

Many Travellers would also attend, to sing or play music or to sell green, white and gold badges with an image of Wolfe Tone on them. One young Traveller from the Liberties, selling his merchandise, recognised Lily and asked her if Wolfe Tone was the favourite jockey. Others sold ballad sheets or played the wheel of fortune, the three-card trick; and dark-shawled women, in hushed tones, would tell people's fortunes. The world and its mother would gather to celebrate the living in true Irish style every bit as much as they would be there to remember the dead.

Most of the marchers, disciplined and well marshalled, would arrive in special trains from Dublin and Cork on the day. They would be accompanied by their favourite pipe bands, with their own provincial banners and decorative colour parties. Both before and after the official march and ceremony, people would be entertained in intimate public house gatherings by songs such as 'The Valley of Knockanure', 'The Boys of Kilmichael', 'Barry's Column', 'A Nation Once Again', 'Kevin Barry', 'Boolavogue', 'Henry Joy McCracken', 'Johnson's Motor Car', 'Whack for the Diddle', or recitations such as 'The Man from God-Knows-Where' and many, many more.

It wasn't always goodwill and comradeship, though, as old animosities could surface easily during the emotional festivities. However, the overall atmosphere would be celebratory and, with the help of strong, sensible women, there was usually enough good sense around to accommodate the peaceful separation of those with serious differences.

Midsummer's day 1931 was a very different affair. That year, the Cosgrave government was engaged in a policy of repression and decided to ban the annual Bodenstown commemoration. It had been planned by the republicans and Fianna Fáil supporters as a major assembly to demonstrate their increased strength in the country and their opposition to the surviving Free State establishment. But a ring of steel was drawn around Sallins and Bodenstown, with armed military, soldiers and officers, and a large contingent of Civic Guards and Special Branch detectives. Many supporters of the event were arrested, or prevented from travelling, earlier in the day, so as to reduce the attendance. de Valera did not attend, but he was thought to be waiting in the wings to see what would happen.

The organisers changed their plans and encouraged people to find alternative ways to approach the area, not to rely on the usual modes of public transport and avoid places where they could be easily arrested. To everyone's surprise, thousands flocked to Wolfe Tone's grave – in such numbers and in such good humour that the authorities were overwhelmed. They were completely unable to hold back the crowds and certainly could not resort to the use of arms to do so.

Seán Russell had been billed as the main speaker but had been arrested during the night. Despite the widespread public hostility to 'Reds', the main speaker was Peadar O'Donnell, frequently attacked as a dangerous communist – something he never was, but he was a staunch and unapologetic republican. In fact, Peadar never even referred to himself as a socialist, preferring the title of 'social Fenian'. In the secret world of the hidden republic, Peadar was a member of the IRA Army Council and Executive, but an opponent of any return to bomb and bullet republicanism. He had also remained a personal friend of de Valera and supported the push to elect Fianna Fáil as the party most likely to remove the Cosgrave government. He took the view that while Dev was strong on constitutional and sovereignty questions, he remained a cautious conservative on social and class issues.

Peadar estimated that between ten and fifteen thousand people had managed to crush into the Bodenstown churchyard, in spite of the ban, to hear him speak on that historic occasion. The remarkable attendance convinced him that republican Ireland had certainly recovered from the Civil War and was seeking new ways to express itself. This renewal of faith in Wolfe Tone's republic had taken place in spite of repression, denunciation from the pulpits and anti-red smear campaigns from the press. O'Donnell took the opportunity to emphasise the importance of both political and social struggles in progressing forward to the desired republic. His point on that day was that every strike for pay, every land struggle, every resistance to land annuities, every demand for housing, jobs or human rights was part of the journey to the desired republic.

His address was enthusiastically received and perceived as a public expression of a policy being advocated, generally behind closed doors, by Peadar himself, George Gilmore, Frank Ryan, Seán Murray, David Fitzgerald and other republicans of the left, but it was not fully embraced by the majority of the IRA leadership. They had a general aversion to engagement in 'politics, even that of Sinn Fein', because of their continued attachment to physical force, as the only way to achieve their objectives.

While Seán Russell also kept in close contact with Dev, he had a very different perspective from Peadar O'Donnell or Dev on the role of the IRA. He sought German support for the IRA during World War II and died aboard a German submarine off the coast of Galway.

Another event in 1931 that was to have a major influence on the political life of this island was the formation of the Free State Army Comrades Association. This body was an unofficial auxiliary to the police, which had direct associations with the officers and men who had suppressed the republicans during and after the Civil War. While it had no legal status, it was closely aligned with the Cumann na nGaedheal party of W.T. Cosgrave. Some people referred to it as 'the White Army', probably a reflection of its ultra-right credentials.

The views of W.T. Cosgrave himself on people who were poor, disadvantaged or dispossessed had been very clearly set out in a letter written in 1921, when he was Minister for Local Government, to Austin Stack:

> *People reared in workhouses, as you are aware, are no great acquisition to the community and they have no ideas whatsoever of civic responsibilities. As a rule, their highest aim is to live at the expense of the ratepayers. Consequently, it would be a decided gain if they all took it into their heads to emigrate. When they go abroad they are thrown on their own responsibilities and have to work whether they like it or not.*

Similarly, during the Civil War, W.T. Cosgrave is quoted (by Garvin, in his 1922 book) as saying:

> I am not going to hesitate and if the country is to live and we have to exterminate 10,000 republicans, the 3 million of our people are bigger than this 10,000.

Later, in the 1930s, in the attacks on Connolly House and the Workers' College in Mrs Despard's house, the mobs were marshalled by men wearing the white armlets of the Army Comrades Association. On some occasions, shots and missiles were fired into the premises of Connolly House and considerable violence was used against those associated with the college. The leader of the organisation was Tom

O'Higgins, brother of Kevin O'Higgins, the former Minister for Justice, who in 1927 had been shot near his home in Blackrock, County Dublin by three members of the IRA in an opportunistic attack.

Later the ACA changed its name to the National Guard and expanded its membership considerably from among the supporters of the Free State in response to the growing support for Fianna Fáil. It attracted considerable support from former soldiers, Irish and British, and from police, business people and large farmers, who feared that the change of political power would endanger their privileged positions and lead to some fearful recrimination for controversial activities during and after the Civil War.

In April 1933, the organisation adopted a uniform of blue shirts, supposedly St Patrick's blue. Its members expressed their admiration for Mussolini's Blackshirts and made no secret of their support for the rising fascist movements in other European states. They also drew public intellectual support and ideology from supporters of the corporate state concept, such as Professor Michael Tierney of UCD, Ernest Blythe, former Minister for Finance, and reputedly W.B. Yeats, who was writing marching songs for them.

When de Valera removed Eoin O'Duffy as Chief Commissioner of the Garda Síochána, the former Chief of Staff of the Free State Army (in 1922) became the leader of the Blueshirts. His second-in-command was Commandant Cronin, also a former senior officer of the Free State Army. Cronin claimed that the organisation's membership numbered 100,000, but O'Duffy claimed a more modest figure of 25,000. Given the members had military training and discipline – and many of them also had a background in the armed police – de Valera had good reason to be anxious. He was also uncertain about the loyalty of existing state forces. He speeded up the recruitment of former IRA members into the Gardaí Special Branch, but unofficially, although it was never admitted, he was also relying on the existence of a large Sinn Féin and IRA membership willing to resist any attempted coup d'état by the now ousted pro-Treaty leadership.

Tom and many other republican comrades in Dublin took the threat so seriously that they had already procured arms and ammunition from local IRA arms dumps. They shared an expectation that they would have to fight a fascist-type attempt to overturn the election results. For many of them, this was no longer simply the old Civil War divisions resurfacing, but a much more immediate threat of a right-wing fascist dictatorship which would seek to crush the trade unions and any other representatives of the underprivileged classes. The unemployed in the cities and the landless rural workers were already experiencing persistent poverty and destitution. While the IRA had not yet taken a formal lead against the Blueshirts, there was spontaneous resistance by their members to this fascist-type threat in all parts of the State.

In August of that year, O'Duffy announced that he was organising a mass parade of Blueshirts, from all parts of the country, to the Griffith–Collins–O'Higgins Memorial on the lawn of Leinster House. Given the proximity of the memorial to the seat of government and the increasingly threatening behaviour of European fascists, de Valera's government reacted by banning the march and proclaiming the National Guard an illegal organisation. Ironically, they revived the Public Safety Act of 1931, with its military tribunals, with which O'Duffy himself had been intimately associated, to address the challenge to the Fianna Fáil government.

An Phoblacht, the republican newspaper, proclaimed on 12 August, before the IRA leadership had actually made up their minds, that:

The people must be aroused as to the conspiracy which is being organised against them. The anti-national and social reactionary character of the interests, of which the fascists are but the mouth piece, must be laid bare. Into the fight against them must be brought the people they propose to enslave. It is the mass of the people which must be organised for action. No police force can take their place. In every district local leadership must become active against the reactionary movement.

Within a short period, Cumann na nGaedheal, the Centre Party (mainly farmers and former Unionists) and O'Duffy's National Guard amalgamated to become 'United Ireland', which they translated as

Fine Gael. O'Duffy was the president and Cosgrave, James Dillon and Frank McDermott were the vice-presidents of the new movement.

By this change of name, O'Duffy sought to keep his organisation within the law, for short intervals, but he continued to organise public rallies that frequently descended into chaotic street fighting, leading to some deaths and many injuries. Most people recognised O'Duffy's tactics as an attempt to reverse the progress of Fianna Fáil and restore the Free State establishment to power by undemocratic means.

In this period of turmoil, Peadar O'Donnell, Frank Ryan, George Gilmore, Michael Price and others of the IRA left wing believed that with the right social policies and clear political direction they could be a major player in a rejuvenation of the political struggle for their lost republic. De Valera met Moss Twomey, Chief of Staff of the IRA, and George Gilmore and outlined his political strategy for achieving the republic. He urged them to disband the IRA and become part of the Irish Defence Forces. They did not accept his suggestion, but it was clear that de Valera had won the political battle and was now determined to consolidate his position as the leader of a constitutional Irish republicanism.

Having dealt with the threat from the 'Free Staters', he set about reducing the potential threat from his own former comrades in Sinn Féin and the IRA. He had stolen their politics and left them only with their guns. The IRA split began at a convention on St Patrick's Day 1934, held in Stephen's Green, at a ballet school, with the most left-inclined delegates among them leaving to form the Republican Congress. This body was formally constituted at a conference that took place in Athlone on 8 April.

The Republican Congress published a successful newspaper, organised branches in many areas, including in Northern Ireland and particularly in Belfast. At first it appeared to have a great future in leading campaigns on employment, industry, housing, health, banking and agriculture. It attracted trade unionists, former labour supporters and republicans alike; Catholic, Protestant, Dissenter; and those with other religious or secular beliefs.

Like many such organisations of the left, it quickly divided on the issue of whether its objective should be a workers' republic or simply a republic. O'Donnell argued for a republic while Michael Price, Roddy Connolly and Nora Connolly argued for a workers' republic. O'Donnell was supported by Seán Murray and Tommy Geehan from Belfast. That early division severely weakened the organisation and although it continued to organise for a few years, it lost a lot of trade union support and failed to rally the majority of republicans to its cause.

In Northern Ireland, political loyalties were also showing signs of strain because of serious economic pressures on workers and their families during the depression of the early thirties. The Northern Irish Unionist leaders had a lot of sympathy with the fascists in Europe and shared with them a generally anti-worker sentiment. In 1934, Sir Oswald Mosley visited Lord Craigavon in Belfast for the purpose of extending his British Fascist movement. It's understood that Craigavon informed him that he already had a fascist force with the Special Constabulary, so there was no need for Mosley to extend his organisation to Northern Ireland.

The Northern government had successfully used sectarianism to secure what it believed was an unassailable position of power. Yet, in the depths of the terrible depression of 1932, it decided to cut the relief rates. It then mobilised the police and military to smash the protests by workers and the unemployed against their starvation payments on relief schemes. A twenty-two-year-old Betty Sinclair led tens of thousands from Ardoyne and Crumlin, from the Falls and Shankill, Protestant and Catholic, to converge at the traditional Custom House steps for a protest meeting.

Within a week of the police and military appearing on the streets, working-class areas of Belfast became battlegrounds against the forces of the State. Barricades were erected against armoured cars and republicans and loyalists were actively united in resisting the forces of the Crown. The Belfast Trades Council called for a general strike and three thousand armed police were brought into Belfast. Trade union officials issued an appeal to workers not to be drawn into sectarian division, as this was a fight against destitution.

The *Irish Press* reported on 12 October: 'Cordon around Belfast. No entry without permission. Street fighting in widely dispersed areas, especially in the Falls and Shankill areas.' A Protestant worker,

John Baxter, and a man named John Geehan were shot dead. It was estimated that a hundred thousand people lined their funeral routes. Within two weeks the government realised that its over-confidence had resulted in the unthinkable unity of Catholics and Protestants in a common struggle for their basic rights. The miserable sum of eight shillings for a man and wife on relief work was raised immediately to 24 shillings.

It was not long before sectarianism was to take hold again, but for some the memory of this short-lived unity was something that republicans only dreamed of. There were valiant efforts by trade union and workers' groups to sustain the class unity in the years that followed, but they met with only limited success.

There were also efforts by the Irish Republican Congress and the James Connolly Club, which came to Bodenstown to march to Wolfe Tone's grave in 1934, to consolidate that unity of purpose, but they were not welcomed by the IRA leadership, who formed a cordon to prevent them marching unless they kept their banners furled. George Gilmore wrote:

> *The Belfast men came as representatives of Republican Congress groups and their banners bore the words, 'Wolfe Tone Commemoration 1934, Shankill Road Belfast Branch, Break the Connection with Capitalism', 'James Connolly Club, Belfast' and United Irishmen of 1934. It was then I heard a shout that I fear will hardly be heard again at Sallins: 'Come On the Shankill' as they battled their way to lay a wreath on Wolfe Tone's grave. Many of the IRA lads broke ranks and came and marched with the Congress groups. After that it was an easy descent into the purely destructive bombing campaigns and the association with Hitler in Europe and O'Duffy in Ireland.*

5

Taking Liberties

It would be difficult to imagine anywhere else in Ireland where ancient and modern history cast as many dark shadows as in Cornmarket, which links High Street to Thomas Street, in the general area of Dublin's Liberties. This was the home of the Geraghty family from the early thirties. It's a place where the ghosts of the past still walk and where ancient history infects the ether. It's part of the original high ridge of defensive land above the River Liffey where the city of Dubh Linn was built by the Norsemen – a part of the original High Street of the medieval city.

Cornmarket is also remarkably close to the ancient meeting place of the island, where the old Gaelic trails met, linking north, south and west. Slí Chualann ran to the south, Slí Dhála to the south-east and west, Slí Mhór to the west and Slí Mhiodhluachra to the north, all fanning out from that hillock above the historic crossing-point of the Liffey. This whole area and community were unceremoniously completely demolished in the 1950s and 1960s by Dublin Corporation so as to create a wider, and highly questionable, route for motor cars to sweep down Bridge Street to the River Liffey.

For many centuries, people had lived and worked here, just above the ancient location of Átha Cliath, the Ford of the Hurdles. Here was the most easterly crossing-point of Abha na Life, the Gaelic name of the River Liffey, from which James Joyce and others derived 'Anna

Livia'. It was also the place that gave its Gaelic name to the city, Baile Átha Cliath.

Cornmarket was the original location of the city's dreaded Newgate Prison, demolished in 1839. This was one of the most important entry points to the markets and trading areas inside the walls of the old city. The gate itself was part of the stone-walled defences of the older Anglo-Norman city, built to keep the native Irish at a safe distance, generally outside the walls; however, they were allowed in at limited times, to trade and to supply fresh agricultural products to the city's inhabitants.

The Black Dog was a notorious name also given to both the prison and to a local tavern. Built by Richard I, it had four towers serving as both a prison and a guarded city gate. The prison was used in the Middle Ages for the imprisonment of many Catholic clerics, including Oliver Plunkett, the Archbishop of Armagh. However, most of the undoubtedly reluctant customers were apparently unfortunate debtors, incarcerated until they could raise enough money to pay for their liberation. Some remnants of these original walls can be seen to this day, between Cornmarket and Lamb Alley.

The Geraghty family lived in number 3 Cornmarket, in one of a block of tenement houses in an advanced state of decay, propped up by a small series of shops supplying sweets and fresh dairy products, a commercial hardware office and some stores. This block, since demolished, was situated virtually at the top of the Forty Steps. It was adjacent to the original Saint Audoen's Protestant Church, built between 1181 and 1212, and an old graveyard, now a park, along the city wall and beside Winstanley House. Along High Street, a larger and more dominant presence is now the more modern Catholic Saint Audeon's (1841–1846), which rises majestically above the older church, the burial yard and High Street. It is a massive grey pillared chapel, a major monument to the latter-day Catholic Church's pre-eminence in the area, built just before the Famine in 1846, in a formerly Protestant locality of the city.

Number 7 Cornmarket was the home of Napper Tandy, one of the most prominent leaders of the United Irishmen, who sought support from France for the 1798 Rebellion and whose house features in the well-known Dublin street ballads 'The Wearing of the Green' and 'The Spanish Lady'.

The Forty Steps leads down from Cornmarket to Saint Audeon's Arch, one of the last remaining gates of the old city. In earlier times, they were the commonly used steps from the respectable heights of High Street to Cook Street and to the lowest depths of 'Hell'. This was the nickname given to the notorious area of ill-repute, known for its taverns, routing houses, wild women, brawls and prostitution. Close by, on Cook Street, it is said you could buy yourself a second-hand coffin, if you needed one.

The Backlane, Lamb Alley and Bridge Street adjoined Cornmarket, each with their many interesting stories to tell. A Backlane gurrier was a title reserved for particularly tough street fighters, although most people there in living memory were decent and law-abiding citizens. This humble lane remains the location of the Tailors' Hall, one of the last remaining guild halls in Dublin, situated in an area that was once a thriving centre for all the old Dublin trade guilds.

The Tailors' Hall was also the meeting place of the historic Catholic Convention, which met in 1792 under the auspices of Wolfe Tone and the United Irishmen, to campaign for the rights of Catholics to vote and to participate in jury service. Bridge Street had the Brewer's Club and led down to an area known as Mullinahack – Muileann an Caca in Gaelic. Lamb Alley was the unofficial street football pitch for the local lads when the guards weren't around. It was also the way to the Iveagh Market, Winstanley's Shoe and Leather Works and the artisan dwelling houses of John Dillon Street. A significant portion of the old city wall is also there to be seen in the alley.

This was the daily route for the Geraghty boys to 'Franner', the Christian Brothers' school they attended in Francis Street after their earlier schooling in Saint Audeon's National School above the ancient city gate or the Masters on School House Lane. Lamb Alley also had the distinction of having a working 'city street-farm' which kept pigs, hens, and an assortment of other animals, not such an unusual type of farm in those days.

That enterprise contributed very significantly to the practical economic life of the young street urchins, who often had a desperate job to raise the essential four pennies for the 'Tivo', more correctly the Tivoli Cinema. It served up an exciting weekly diet of cowboy films on Saturday afternoons, a very popular event for the local children. Buckets of waste food were a great source of revenue – the city farm usually paid a penny for each full bucket of waste food supplied. This meant it only took four visits to accumulate the price of a ticket to the 'pics'. Otherwise you might have to gather rags, bottles or jam-jars for sale to the more distant Isaacson's store in Kevin Street.

Cornmarket was originally the place where large amounts of corn were traded and it had a building called the Corn Premium Office. That trade inevitably brought much wider agricultural trading activities to the area. It was also the location of the Bull Ring and a famous stone was located there for many years, with a strong iron ring for attaching bulls. In the Middle Ages, it was one of the places where the city's watchmen were charged to ensure that at night 'no Irish man or men with beards above the mouth to be lodged within the city'. By parliamentary decree, the city authorities demanded that 'no Englishman shall have hairs on his upper lip and any Irishman with an emigrant look should be brought to the city's Mayor'.

By the sixteenth century, the once English and Protestant city of Dublin had certainly acquired a very distinct 'Irish' look, with 1,180 pubs and 91 public breweries, many located in this part of the city and around the Liberties. George Bernard Shaw, himself a Dubliner, blamed the Irish weather for the temperament of the Irish, which, he maintained, 'will stamp an emigrant more deeply and durably in two years, apparently, than the English climate will in two hundred'. Another more likely explanation for the Dublin fondness for alcohol might be that it was frequently a safer drink for humans than the polluted water then available for consumption.

Tom Geraghty senior, who worked in the stores of Huggard's at 3–5 Cornmarket, also had a great interest in local history and imparted that to his five sons. They were all born in the old Coombe Hospital and spent their early years in the house, above the stores at number 3. From the back window they could see the rooftop and granite structure of the Four Courts, across on the north side of the Liffey, the scene of intense fighting in both 1916 and 1922. Not only were the young Geraghtys acquainted with the building, but they knew who commanded and who defended the Four Courts on each occasion. They also learned where the British Army artillery, given to the Free State Army in 1922, was dug in. One old local, a former veteran gunner in the British Army called Paddy Whack, claimed to have been recruited in 1922 to help blast the 'Shinners' out of the Four Courts, because the Free State gang didn't know how to use their big guns properly.

On visits across the river, Tom's boys were also shown the bullet holes and scars of war on the masonry of the surviving building. Tom, himself a great city walker, would take them on regular rambles to Arbour Hill, Boland's Mill, South Dublin Union, Glasnevin Cemetery, Dublin Castle and the GPO. They were introduced to such historic places as the College of Surgeons in Stephen's Green, where Michael Mallon and Countess Markievicz of the Irish Citizen Army fought in 1916; and Jacob's Factory, close by, where Peadar Kearney was a member of the garrison and refused to surrender to the British military at the end of the week's hostilities. During their childhood, Jacob's biscuit factory was a great place for bargains, like bags of broken biscuits, sold cheaply to staff and locals; but it was also remembered as the place where Rosie Hackett organised the union and featured in the 1916 Rebellion.

It could be said that the whole Geraghty family was reared lovingly by Tom and Lily on a wholesome diet of self-confidence, cabbage and potatoes, porridge, native pride, class consciousness and social revolution. They were always encouraged to read books, the poor person's education; and to enjoy music, ballads, stories and, on very special occasions, the theatre, or concerts, if tickets could be secured cheaply or for free. The library in Thomas Street was used regularly, as were cheap books bought from book-barrows around the city. Lily particularly loved the opera, as did her son Séamus, and they were lucky enough to have a local neighbour, Mick Gill, who worked as an attendant in the Gaiety Theatre and would often secure complementary tickets for both of them. Des acquired a clerk's tin whistle and set about entertaining himself with bits and scraps of local music and street songs. He loved to listen to the many buskers who frequented the area.

Tom was a hard-working father, who had little interest in drink or public houses. He spent most of his spare time developing a magical and productive garden, an invaluable resource he had painstakingly developed on a rough piece of waste ground between the back of the house and the old Dublin city wall, overlooking Cook Street. From that fertile patch, he produced an amazing range of fresh produce: cabbage and potatoes, scallions, carrots, pods of peas, gooseberries, radishes and fruit of all descriptions. Rhubarb was his particular speciality, and Lily would make rhubarb and custard, rhubarb jam and rhubarb tarts in abundance, which could be consumed by the family and shared generously with neighbours and friends. This produce proved an invaluable asset for all concerned during the difficult and frugal years of the National Emergency, 1939–1945. It was a haven of peace and nature's harvest that Tom created for the family.

On the day his son Desmond was born in October 1943, Tom planted a sycamore tree, which outgrew Des to such an extent that he learned to climb on its branches with love and enthusiasm and to enjoy the leaves, flowers and shrubs all around him in the garden.

One of the secrets of Tom's horticultural success was his strategic positioning of a wooden box-car with a garden shovel behind the front door of his hardware stores. There the city's horse carters had to deliver their cargo of hardware goods, while their large dray horses took the opportunity to discharge their own heavy load of steaming horse manure. Tom never failed to secure this gift of nature's riches, with the assistance of a bucket of water which helped to keep the street's kerbs and cobblestones clean after removing the valuable gift.

Given the largely republican background of the family, it was considered a very courageous and controversial decision when Tom joined the Free State Local Defence Force, the LDF, and became a convenor for the Liberties. Some members of Lily's family had yet to recognise the institutions of the Free State and considered the illegal IRA as the only legitimate army of the republic. Her elder brother Jim, Séamus O'Néill, was involved with other officers of Sinn Féin in a court action taken in 1942 against the de Valera government in respect of the Sinn Féin funds, held in trust in the High Court since 1924. Jim's two sons, Mattie and Christy, were interned in the Curragh Camp during the war years, along with Brendan Behan, Máirtín Ó Cadhain and hundreds of other republicans and socialists.

Tom had made up his mind that Ireland and people of the left in Ireland had more to fear from a German invasion than a British one and he was determined to play his part in resisting such an event. He recalled with humour how, when German forces bombed the North Strand on the night of Friday 31 May 1942, the volunteers of the LDF were called up, with Tom's help, for an assembly in Skipper's Alley in the Liberties. To the consternation of the senior officers, some of the supposedly fully equipped soldiers, there to defend their country, arrived with six-packs of Guinness in their military haversacks. Tom jokingly pointed out that it was obvious they thought there might be a very serious scrap with the Germans, so they brought their best available medication with them.

Sometimes people can have romantic notions about the 'Rebel Liberties' but in truth there was serious poverty and deprivation in the area at that time. Unemployment was rampant, which led to emigration and, for some, service in the British Army. Despite the hardships and deprivation, the people retained a strong sense of community spirit. Tuberculosis, a constant scourge, was not addressed properly for many years in the area.

Neighbours generally helped each other out and shared the little they had. The biggest problem was the poor quality of the older tenement houses and the health and hygiene issues associated with them. There remains a sturdy stock of modest redbrick artisan dwellings in John Dillon Street and surrounding areas. Similarly there are some in Saint Audeon's Terrace; also a whole Iveagh Trust development on Bride Street, Ross Road, Nicolas Street and Patrick Street, from Christ Church Place right down to Saint Patrick's Cathedral. The Iveagh buildings were a legacy of the Guinness Brewery and one might now wonder why the wealthy multinational enterprises have not been asked to contribute more to resolving the current housing problems, in part created by their success in sucking thousands of employees into the city and neighbourhood of Dublin.

Within that impressive Iveagh complex was the Bayno, a wonderful institution of immense value for poor children, with swimming baths, a night shelter and playground; and the only off-street space for playing football after school. The decent women of that institution provided lovely soft yellow currant buns and mugs of hot Shell cocoa for all who ventured there.

All five of Tom and Lily's boys attended 'Low and High Babies' in the old Saint Audoen's national school situated just above the old Saint Audeon's Arch, at the bottom of the Forty Steps. That was the early schoolhouse for the entry of young children to formal education before graduating to 'the Masters', situated on School House Lane off High Street.

Big Don and Little Don, the name of card games, were the nick-names of the two schoolmasters who administered 'the Masters'. They were rough enough characters, who didn't spare the cane when they considered that corporal punishment was appropriate. The Geraghtys later graduated to Francis Street Christian Brothers' School, because Tom was a Christian Brothers boy himself and had great faith in their schools. But his boys discovered soon enough that the Brothers had their own methods for imposing learning on reluctant pupils.

Thanks to the wonderful Miss Leonard and Miss Gleeson in the Junior School, the children received a great start in their early education. Resources were very limited, so these dedicated teachers improvised with slates and chalk, wooden thread spools, beads for counting, coloured strings, painted polish tins, long matchsticks and a variety of shells and stones from the seaside. The walls were festooned with the pupils' artworks – posters painted on butchers' wrapping paper, wallpaper and cardboard. Best of all, those teachers never used any form of corporal punishment or made any distinction between their pupils. They just encouraged their learning, with fun, games and singing as their preferred teaching methods. They also introduced the children to the Irish language, with practical phrases like *Tá mé ag siúl; Tá mé ag dul abhaile; Téigh a chodladh; Dúisigh; An bhfuil cead agam dul amach?; Slán leat; Fáilte romhat.*

That school had been in existence since the 1750s, when it was called St Audoen's Roman Catholic Free School. Apparently the 'Free' referred to the official independence of the school from the parish, as it was run by a lay committee. During its long and eventful history, it made an important contribution to the education of the local population. One of its earliest pupils was a dramatist named John O'Keeffe, who wrote 68 plays, pantomimes, comedies and farces. His most famous play was *Wild Oats*, which was revived by the Royal Shakespeare Company in London in 1976 and ran for two years. It was also performed at Dublin's Abbey Theatre in 1977. This former pupil was considered to be the most popular dramatist in the English-speaking world in the second half of the eighteenth century.

Another of the attendees was Peadar Kearney, the author of the Irish national anthem, 'The Soldier's Song', and a volunteer in Jacob's Factory in the 1916 Easter Rising. Earlier, in 1910, as part of a campaign to extend the 1906 School Meals Act to Ireland, such famous women as Helena Moloney, Maud Gonne MacBride and Countess Markievicz, as well as Grace, Muriel and Sydney Gifford, served up school dinners from the Penny Dinners in Meath Street for the pupils in St Audoen's School. This was part of a pilot project to demonstrate how such a scheme could function in the poorer schools in Dublin.

One of the more famous pupils of the same school, in relatively recent years, was the most decorated police officer in the United States, John F. Timoney, one of the first pupils in the new school in Cook Street. He pioneered the phrase in policing 'zero tolerance', which he applied vigorously to criminals in New York City as first Deputy Police Commissioner. He later became Police Commissioner for Philadelphia and Chief of Police in Miami. It may be that he was influenced by the quick-fisted policing model applied by Lugs Brannigan and his 'heavy gang' to the more minor law-breakers on the streets of the Liberties.

An early fear which had to be overcome by the very young children was that of passing, every day, the dark, forbidding and supposedly haunted entrance to the ancient Saint Audoen's graveyard, immediately adjoining the entrance to the children's school on the Forty Steps. Older people in the neighbourhood believed that a 'Green Lady' frequented this dark place, combed her long hair there and had a comb that could kill anyone who had the temerity to come close enough to her throwing distance:

On the steps of St Audoen's I heard yer sad wailing,
I knew what ails ye, I never could tell,
A beautiful lady for a loved one still grieving
Or a poor creature lost between Heaven and Hell?
Green Lady, Green Lady, they say that they saw you,
Dancing in the moonlight and combing your hair,
Spreading your charms on the cold Winter's evening,
Enticing poor mortals to come to your lair.

Curiously, apart from the mythology surrounding the Green Lady, it was known for many years earlier that a small door did exist on the Forty Steps, at the back of the old St Audoen's Church, where deserted babies could be left by distraught parents, to be rescued by the Church authorities, possibly for adoption or simply for survival. The adjoining park was at times frequented by people sleeping rough or 'out on gur' (an old term for living on your wits, or away from home).

There was a small bit of shelter in the structure above Saint Audoen's Arch, where a 'Johnny Forty Coats' could take shelter from the elements. The well-known Bang-Bang was often a passing visitor, to the delight of the kids, although he never delayed too long from his insatiable quest for wild Indians or lawless cowboys hanging out on High Street, Cornmarket or Thomas Street. He preferred the use of passing Ballyfermot buses as a 'covered wagon' to give him cover from his pursuers while he shot them down with a deadly 'bang-bang' from his brass pretend shooter.

That harmless cowboy game-play was far removed from that of the street wars associated with the Liberties in earlier centuries. In those times, there were often deadly confrontations between the Liberty Boys and the Ormond Boys from the Northside of the river. John Edward Walsh in his book *Rakes and Ruffians*, wrote that in the 1790s:

Among the lower orders, a feud and deadly hostility had
grown up between the Liberty Boys, or tailors and weavers of
the Coombe, and the Ormond Boys, or butchers who lived in
Ormond Market, on Ormond Quay, which caused frequent
conflicts; and it is in the memory of many now living that

the streets, and particularly the quays and bridges, were impassable in consequence of the battles of these parties.

Growing up in the Liberties of Dublin in the 1940s and 1950s had its own risks, maybe not comparable with the violent battles between the Liberty Boys and the Ormond Boys of old, but sometimes very serious nevertheless. There were some street skirmishes among young people which could turn nasty if particular gangs became involved. Violence and threatening behaviour were not confined to any particular area of the city, but were clearly more extensive in poorer working-class communities where the scourges of poverty, unemployment and other social ills were constantly prevalent.

Each of the Geraghtys learned that having five strong and sturdy brothers in the one family was a distinct advantage. In minor confrontations with local street gangs or even with schoolyard bullies, the immediate back-up of four tough brothers was an invaluable safeguard. The more ominous presence was the so-called 'Animal Gangs', who were to be avoided at all costs or left to the police 'heavy gang' to be dealt with.

Tom and Lily were no strangers to conflict, so they generally encouraged and instilled self-reliance and street savvy in all the boys. It was normal for them to have a self-reliant response to most threatening situations. If that was not sufficient, they would never hesitate to weigh in with full support for the family, right or wrong. With that understanding, the boys all survived very well and loved living in the Liberties.

Unfortunately, circumstances changed in the mid-1950s when the Huggard family decided to dispense with Tom's services after twenty-three years of loyal service. After months of heart-breaking unemployment, he secured a caretaker's job in the Health Clinic in Drimnagh and eventually located a nearby house to rent, which enabled the whole family to migrate from the city to the alien suburb of Drimnagh. The boys generally regretted leaving the Liberties although they recognised that the new home was a necessity for Tom and his work, and they were aware that the corporation intended to demolish the whole block of houses in Cornmarket at an early date.

Lily's fighting spirit never diminished with age. Des, who was a clingy son, has very fond memories of her regular challenges to shopkeepers about overcharging. She was a proud member of the Irish Housewives Association and wore her badge on all shopping expeditions. Every butcher or grocer in the area needed to know what they were charging for every ounce of meat or groceries. In the butcher's shop, she would ask them to pour off any excess water or reduce any bulky packaging before she accepted their price. Equally, the fishmongers had to clean off any ice before weighing their fish; and no dealer would get away with selling her damaged fruit. She knew everywhere that a bargain could be had and carefully timed shopping for meat and fish at just before closing time. She knew when the shopkeepers would want to sell off the day's stock at a reduced price, because fridges were uncommon in those days. She knew remarkably well how to share an egg and how to transform two single fish and chips from Burdock's chipper into a meal for seven.

A worrying development in the Liberties in the 1940s and 1950s was the very serious increase in the incidence of tuberculosis, the dreaded TB. No family was safe from the onslaught of that dreaded disease, which was highly infectious and clearly exacerbated by the dampness and unhygienic conditions in the older houses of the area. The air, polluted by coal and damp turf smoke, did not help; nor did poor diet and lack of protective clothing during inclement weather. This was essentially a deadly disease of the poor.

It was not uncommon to see children going barefoot on the streets at that time. On the first day of school in Francis Street, Des was asked to bring three barefoot children to Benson's shoe shop in Cornmarket, to be provided with shoes paid for by vouchers from the Herald Boot Fund. These were made available by the teachers in the school as part of a public project to protect barefoot children.

Wellington boots with holes and leaky leather boots were so common that chilblains were a common scourge for children in winter, and when TB reared its ugly head, the existing health services were entirely inadequate for the task required. As a consequence, the name of one particular politician rang out loud and clear in the Cornmarket family household. That name was Dr Noël Browne TD. He was regarded highly by the people, not so much as a radical politician but as a miracle-worker, willing to do whatever was necessary to beat the dreadful disease of TB. For that and many other reasons Noël Browne was strongly supported by all of the Geraghty family in later years.

6

Songs and Rhythms from the Cobblestones

In the dark, unlit hall of the house in Cornmarket, young Des, on a late evening, could see a trickle of light under the door of Mr Conway's room. This light was accompanied by a gentle stream of fiddle music, which seemed to flow from beneath the door and sail on the golden stream of light, expanding into a wave of magical sound, reverberating all around in the dark expanse of the high-ceilinged hallway. It sucked him into a new, mysterious place. Surely this was the magic music of the gods, or the sidhe, an ancient sound that stirred the imagination and awoke the heart to a sense of ancient mystical places, past memories and unexplored dreams.

The quiet, unassuming Mr Conway, who Des's mother Lily referred to as Micksey, was an elderly Tipperary man who spoke very little, coming and going unobtrusively to and from his room on the first floor of the house. He was obviously very religious, as Des had seen him regularly going out to evening 'devotions' in some church or other. There were at least seven such churches in close proximity to Cornmarket, which made the annual religious 'Seven Churches' ritual easy to accomplish. Des also knew that their quiet neighbour moulded small religious statues in his room, as Lily often had to clear the residual clay dust from the hall outside his door. Otherwise he was a kind of mystery man who rarely spoke and, apart from playing an old fiddle quietly in his room, never disturbed anyone in the rest of the house. Lily would occasionally help him dump some rubbish, or share some of her home-baked tarts with him.

It was the mellow sound of his fiddle music that lingered deep in Des's memory. It's often assumed that traditional music and song belonged only to rural Ireland, but that was not the case – the city had its own store of musical wonder, maybe drawn from many diverse and distant directions, yet adapted, played and enjoyed by many city dwellers, young and old.

Song and music were not unknown in the Geraghty household. Lily had a rich store of old songs and on occasion would play her mouth organ for fun. The family also had an old wind-up gramophone in the front room with a mixed selection of old 78s – His Master's Voice and other labels. Paul Robeson was the favourite, with his spirituals, extracts from the opera and 'Old Man River' from the musicals. John McCormack songs were also well represented, as was 'Emmett's Speech from the Dock' and Constance Markievicz's 'Battle Hymn of the Republic', the Kincora Céilí Band and Michael Coleman's fiddle music recorded in America. However, none of these recordings could compare with the quiet, magical sound of an old, seasoned fiddle heard in the ambience of the dark first-floor hallway of Des's own home.

Street music was a regular feature in their neighbourhood as the Boys' Brigade paraded along their street en route from Church Street, on the north side of the River Liffey, to St Audoen's Church on High Street. St James' Brass and Reed Band would often march past on practice runs and the street would be filled with a great feast of piping and drumming on St Patrick's Day as the many marching bands passed through Cornmarket and High Street and on to Thomas Street and beyond. This was the old route for the parade, which was changed after the family was exiled to the distant suburbs of Drimnagh, when Tom had to change jobs and the City Corporation set about demol-ishing their old street.

In those days before television, there was a great dependence on home entertainment; the radio, the local cinema, the Tivoli; as well as frequent and unpredictable street entertainment. The Tivoli was later owned and restored by Tony Byrne, who was many years before in Des's class in the Christian Brothers School on Francis Street. Cornmarket had a few natural advantages in relation to entertainment as there were two pubs adjacent to each other, in a large, curved space between Backlane and Lamb Alley, which allowed every conceivable hurdy-gurdy, trick-of-the-loop, three-card trickster, fire-eater or pedlar to perform safely, away from passing trucks, carts or motor cars. One pedlar used to offer 'Young men's tricycles, old men's bicycles and guns that shoot around corners' to promote his wares, without even one bicycle in sight.

The value of the two adjoining pubs was that performers could play outside and then make a collection in both premises, a sort of two-for-the-price-of-one. Johnny and Felix Doran were known to play their uilleann pipes there, standing up, with a small wooden support leg placed under one knee. Ted Furey also played the banjo there, before he later adopted the fiddle. There were of course some awful bawdy street singers with great lung power, who would be regularly paid off by the publicans to take themselves elsewhere. In those days, street musicians and singers were rarely allowed into the pubs, unless they were part of a wedding party or involved in a pre-arranged celebration or special event.

The most consistent exposure to street music came from the young girls who had singing and dancing skills to accompany their skipping-rope or ball-game abilities. Tunes like 'Down in the alley O, the alley O, the alley O, where we play relievie-ee-o ...'; 'Down by the River Sawl-ya'; 'Wallflowers, wallflowers, growing up so high'; 'See the robbers passing by, passing by, see the robbers passing by, my fair lady'; or 'Johnson Mooney and O'Brien, bought a horse for one an' nine'; or 'Don't eat Kennedy's bread, it'll stick to your belly like lead'; 'Down by the Lucan dairy'; or 'Lazy Mary will you get up, will you get up, Lazy Mary, will you get up on a cold and frosty morning' were some of the favourites. In the long grass of St Audoen's Park, it was rhythms about the 'Birds and bees, jinny-joes and daffodils, dandelions and daisies' or 'Spin the bottle round and round, until you find your lady'. These familiar children's rhymes were part of a local street tradition which had its own sense of wonderment, which brought out a natural love of music and song, provided hours of fun and enjoyment and brightened up our lives as children. It was free, a part of us, it was our own inheritance, which mothers, sisters and brothers passed on seamlessly. It was never devalued by being sold as a commodity.

The Geraghtys were great radio listeners and the boys loved the radio drama *Perry Mason, Pilot of the Future* on Radio Luxembourg; but every week, it was *The Ballad Makers of Saturday Night* that was the real family favourite. On one occasion, the wonderful lilting western voices of Kerry, Connemara, Donegal or Clare were replaced with the strong Dublin accent of Brendan Behan, well known to the family, introducing the programme:

> *Often on a winter's evening, after tea, all the kids on the street would stand around the lamp on the corner, watching along the road for Billy the Light, to reach the lamp. You could see for a mile up the Circular Road, the lamps going on, one after another as he came nearer. Then at last he was at ours and the little light, that never went out either by day or night, at the touch of a stick would burst the mantle into an orange flame and the singing would start. Songs that were never made on paper, but grew out of the stories of the pavement, passed on from one generation of children to the next, songs that were as old as Zoodlum Zoo, that were sung before Daniel O'Connell when he was well thought of.*

Brendan's mother, Kathleen, a sister of Peadar Kearney, author of the national anthem and many more songs, was a great resource for Brendan and his brother, Dominic, who were steeped in that tradition. Dominic both wrote and adapted a significant number of fine songs and perhaps more than anyone else captured the harsh experience of Irish building workers in the 1950s, 'Building Up and Tearing Old England Down'. Brendan's 'Captains and the Kings' and 'The Laughing Boy' are classic songs from *The Hostage*, Brendan's most successful play. His version of 'The Old Triangle' is one of the best-loved and most widely -sung Dublin songs, although he boasted, that 'I can't read a note of music, but I can certainly read a cheque.'

Many songs and ballads were shared among the republican community through such publications as individual ballad sheets, Walton's song books and a range of Brian O'Higgins's publications. Some of the songs are maudlin, sentimental and of little artistic merit, but others are well written and musical, telling untold stories of significance, in the true rebel spirit of the people. The best of them have become an integral part of our living tradition. Lily O'Neill, the mother of all the Geraghtys, was actually related by marriage to McCall. Her brother Jim's wife was Bridget Whitty from Ballinglen and Bridget and her sister Maggie, who became the housekeeper of the painter Jack B. Yeats, were both related to McCall. Brendan Kennelly, the great Kerry poet and adopted Dubliner, put it well when he said that 'all songs are living ghosts and long for a living voice.'

Des was intrigued by the name of James Clarence Mangan on a redbrick wall close to the Christian Brothers' School in Francis Street. He had learnt that Mangan was a Dublin poet who had lived in the Liberties and was the author of the poem and song 'My Dark Rosaleen'. Des had heard that version of the song sung long before Seán Ó Riada's 'Mise Éire', which was based on the same poem but had a very different and beautiful air. In Mangan's song 'The Nameless One', he wrote the inspiring line 'Roll forth my song, like the rushing river.' Des took a special interest in Mangan's writings and discovered that he had written hundreds of other songs and poems, some from the Gaelic past and some for the Young Ireland movement and *The Nation*. The diverse national and international character of his work, his own sad and tormented life story and his miserable death in 1849 from famine disease in Bride Street, deeply stirred the imagination of the young Geraghty. In his teens, Des wrote his own modest epitaph to Mangan on a small Walton's pamphlet of his songs and poems:

Familiar name on a red brick wall
where heavy shadows of history fall,
Grim grey walls of Church and State
By Dublin Castle and Christ Church Place.
Pilgrim poet who did imbibe
Spirits of the long lost tribes,

Found secret ways to a warmer clime,
Escaped from those, cold cobble stones of mine.

Another Dublin writer who had a special interest in Mangan was the poet and writer P.J. McCall, who was born in Patrick Street in 1861 and died in 1919. McCall, the son of a publican and grocer, was a prolific writer of songs, ballads, poetry and local history, a fluent Irish speaker, composer and fiddle player. He is best remembered for his patriotic ballads such as those relating to the United Irishmen and the Wexford uprising of 1798 – 'Boolavogue', 'The Boys of Wexford', 'Kelly the Boy from Killane', 'Follow Me Up to Carlow', 'The Low Lands Low' – songs that were widely known and have remained an important part of the Irish musical tradition.

McCall wrote pamphlets about Saint Patrick's and Christchurch cathedrals, two of the great cornerstones of that part of Dublin, which for centuries have cast their imposing shadows over the Liberties. He played an important part in the Irish literary and cultural revival of the early twentieth century and was also a passionate advocate for protecting the strong community and cultural riches of the Liberties. Living in Patrick Street, in the shadow of Saint Patrick's, McCall could not escape the intellectual influence and local memory of Dean Swift of Saint Patrick's Cathedral, or the spirit of Zozimus, the vigorous street balladeer from the nearby Faddle Alley, who had also lived in Patrick Street, many years before. Zozimus is the best remembered of many street singers who frequented the Liberties after the Act of Union and Robert Emmet's ill-fated uprising of 1803.

The story of Emmet and his execution inspired many traditional songs and influenced his friend Tom Moore to write fondly of him in songs such as 'When He Who Adores Thee', 'Oh Breathe Not His Name', or 'The Minstrel Boy' with the stirring words, 'thy songs were made for the pure and free and shall never sound in slavery.' These songs of Moore were usually heard in much more salubrious surroundings than those of the Dublin street singers of his time, but nevertheless they form a part of the tradition. The words that Moore wrote for his songs are rooted in the music and melodies of Bunting's Irish airs, which he gleaned from the ancient harpers.

Zozimus, the great street balladeer who boasted that he walked in the footsteps of Homer, wrote such songs as 'The Finding of Moses', 'The Twang Man' and 'Ye Men of Sweet Liberties Hall'. In the latter song, he proclaimed his support for the Liberties as he sang of 'the Coombe and each street, long before the vile Union was known...' and called for the rights of the Liberty Boys and 'its streets with her chapels and schools which retain, a spirit unbroken and bold'.

His last instructions before his death and a requiem to his friends and those who attended him – a room full of ballad singers – is a masterpiece of street lore, recorded by many other musicians including the Reverend Nicholas O'Farrell:

I have no coronet to go before me,
Nor Bucephalus that ever bore me;
But put me hat and gloves together,
That bore for years the very worst of weather,
And rest assured in spirit will be there,
Mary of Agypt and Susannah fair.
And Pharoah's daughter with heavenly blushes,
That took the drowning gosling from the rushes.
I'll not permit a tomb-stone stuck above me,
Nor effigy; but, boys; if still yees love me,
Build a nate house for all whose fate is hard,
And give a bed to every wanderin' bard.

According to William Fitzpatrick's *History of the Cemeteries of Dublin* (1900), Michael Moran, better known as Zozimus, died in 1846, in the middle of the Great Famine. He was only 43 and his death was due to pulmonary disease caused by exposure to severe weather in that year.

Jonathan Swift, the Dean of St Patrick's, who lived in the previous century, was a prolific writer whose works included *Gulliver's Travels*, *Drapier's Letters* and *A Modest Proposal*. He was born in Dublin in 1667 and was appointed to his position as Dean in 1713. He is particularly remembered for exposing England's perfidy in Ireland, most famously in his opposition to Wood's Halfpence, which he saw as an inferior currency, in 1724. Swift was a colossus of the literary world of his day for the clarity of his prose and the sharpness of his wit. He was referred to as the 'Mad Dean' by some of his detractors in the British establishment, but Sir William Wilde, the Dublin surgeon, and Oscar Wilde's father, rejected that view. It was later established that he was certainly not mad, but did suffer from Ménière's disease, a disorder of the inner ear that can lead to dizzy spells and hearing loss. Swift left us with some memorable observations on life, such as 'we have just enough religion to make us hate but not enough to make us love one another.' On politics, he pointed out that 'In all free states, the evil to be avoided is tyranny, that is to say the "summa imperii" or unlimited power solely in the hands of one, the few or the many.' Another shrewd observation of his was 'Vision is the art of seeing things invisible.' The people of the Liberties had many stories about the exploits of the Dean and an unending series of humorous tales, some true and others contrived. But he was greatly loved by the poor people of the Liberties, who he supported and cherished. He was generous with his resources and was owed a lot of money by his many debtors when he died.

The strong egalitarian spirit of those earlier days has since been sustained and recorded over the generations by many writers and poets familiar with the area. Those who readily spring to mind are Máirín Johnson, singer and author of *Around the Banks of Pimlico*, a friend of the Geraghty family, who has played no small role in labour politics and the women's movement over the years. Another is Liam O'Meara, the poet and writer who remembered, among others, the poet Francis Ledwidge, the Bayno, the Iveagh Trust play centre and Zozimus.

Others include Éamonn Mac Thomáis, with his many stories; Frank Hopkins; Lar Redmond; Phil O'Keeffe; Jim Smith; Elgy Gillespie and so many more. Joe O'Connor, Sinéad O'Connor and Imelda May are also of strong Liberties stock, as was Brendan Grace, the wonderful entertainer, comedian and singer. Pete St John's song 'Dublin in the Rare Oul' Times', sung by Luke Kelly in his own inimitable style, is well peopled by citizens of the Liberties. Gerard Smyth, one of our finest poets, draws much inspiration from his knowledge of this part of Dublin.

One night in the Pipers' Club in Thomas Street, Des heard Big Jim Crystal play 'The Blackbird' on the fiddle and was immediately reminded of Micksy Conway and his fiddle music in Number 3, Cornmarket. That was the mystery tune, the one that filled the air so beautifully and created such a strong impression on the young listener. Des knew that Micksy had since become a monk in Mellifont Abbey; and on one occasion, he came to Liberty Hall on his first day's release from that silent institution. He said hello with a very hoarse voice and told Des that he loved the peaceful monastic life as a Cistercian, but in the early days, when he was denied his fiddle, he had felt very sad.

That quiet fiddler was once Commandant Michael Conway of the IRA. He was referred to by Brendan Behan in *Borstal Boy* as the officer of his Fianna camp before embarking on his solo bombing campaign in Britain in 1939. He had lived through dangerous times, had had his own confrontations with death and was party to a tragedy which saw a young Fianna boy lose his life when a loaded revolver was discharged accidently. It was evident that his fiddle and his music were part of his way of mourning, while still celebrating the gift of life and beauty.

7

An Injury to One
Is the Concern of All

Big Jim Larkin, the labour leader, 'the Great Lion of the Fold', died in early 1947, after a short period in the Meath Hospital. He had had an accident in his trade union premises before Christmas, but, in characteristic form, he ignored it. Early in the New Year, he was admitted to hospital where his condition deteriorated rapidly and he died on 30 January. Larkin's death brought out the multitudes onto the streets of Dublin City, as his body was taken from the Meath Hospital to the trade union premises in College Street, where he lay in state for two days. Thousands of his old friends and comrades came to pay their respects to their lost leader before his burial on the bitterly harsh day of 2 February.

Tom paid his own respects to his idol in the union hall in College Street and on the miserable, cold, slushy day of the funeral. He brought his three eldest children – Seán, Tom and Séamus – with him to march behind the coffin on its way to Glasnevin.

Jim Larkin was a controversial figure throughout his life and has been the subject of much detailed historical analysis and debate. When he died, the workers, the poor and downtrodden people of Dublin needed no such analysis. They knew he was their lost leader and they came out instinctively, in spite of the inclement weather, to bid farewell to their hero and friend. Larkin was the one who gave people hope, who lifted them up, challenging their enemies and inviting them to join him in a fight for a bright new world of dignity and respect. They knew he made mistakes, made many enemies, could be criticised for his stubborn personality, his judgement or his tactics in complex and difficult situations. However, they were in no doubt about his importance for their lives, his enduring loyalty to their aspirations and his absolute commitment to the interests of the working class of all nations. His was the fire and brimstone of a 'spiritual revolution' in their darkest hour, far more than any other radical trade union leader. In the early 1900s, his 'divine gospel of discontent was a wake-up call for all the dispossessed, a courageous challenge to their exploiters and a powerful doctrine of freedom and justice for workers. He was Ireland's messiah of the lower orders, who had come to liberate them from their degradation.

In his early years, Des often reflected on the truly spiritual nature of Larkinism. For him, 'an injury to one is the concern of all' was an appeal to a universal concern for all people, far above the concepts of me, or myself (mé féin), or sinn féin (we ourselves, the Irish people). It's a more powerful call to our most important identity, our fundamental humanity. It's that missing ingredient that was so evident to Larkin, as he observed the destructive consequences of man's inhumanity to man in his early life, as a seaman, on the docks of Liverpool, Belfast, Cork and Dublin; and which he passionately wanted to do something about, even at the cost of his own destruction.

'The great only appear great because we are on our knees' is another appeal to a more universal theme, an urge to stand up and claim the full height of your human status. It's another dimension of James Connolly's global declaration, 'Our demands most modest are, we only want the earth.' It also has an echo of Dubliner Oscar Wilde's statement, 'We are all in the gutter, but some of us are looking at the stars.' What could have been a stronger challenge to Dublin employers, who were engaged in the degrading exploitation of poor people, than Larkin's defiant statement about the employers, 'Christ will not be crucified any longer in Dublin by these men'?

Many of our artists, poets and writers have captured that spiritual quality of Larkin's appeal, with different degrees of success. Austin Clarke's 'Inscription on a Headstone' is certainly memorable:

> *His name endures on our holiest page,*
> *scrawled in rage by Dublin's poor.*

As are Paddy Kavanagh's lines on Larkin and the great Lock-Out:

> *... slavery crept to its hands and knees*
> *And nineteen thirteen cheered from out the utter*
> *Degradation of their miseries.*

Seán O'Casey, a great friend and admirer of Larkin, wrote about the powerful appeal of Larkin's voice, which cried out:

> *labour, a gift, not a curse, poetry, dancing and principles ...*
> *here was a man who would put a flower in a vase on a table*
> *as well as a loaf on a plate.*

Perhaps it was Brendan Behan, a radical of a younger generation, who summed it up best for the young Geraghtys in his Gaelic poem as he marched behind Jim Larkin's coffin:

> *Ba mise é! Ba gach mach máthair againn é*
> *Sinn Féin. Láidir. Mar abáil linn a bheith*
> *Mar ab ól dúinn a bheith.*

> *I was him! He was every mother's son of us*
> *Ourselves alone. Strong. As we would love to be*
> *As we would know to be.*

It should be no surprise that in spite of very different temperaments and a variety of opinions among the seven members of the Geraghty household, they were all deeply influenced by Larkinism. All the boys, through many circuitous routes, became trade union representatives and would always defend Larkin from his detractors.

Trade unions, or combinations as they were sometimes called, have a very long history in Dublin and Ireland, dating back many centuries. In spite of being illegal under Irish Acts of Parliament from as early as 1729, the law was largely ignored by workers and employers alike. In parliamentary investigations in 1824 and 1838 it was acknowledged that 'the Dublin trades were the best organised in the Kingdom', but most MPs were landlords or their agents and were hostile to all forms of combinations that they did not control.

Many of the Dublin guilds were located in the vicinity of High Street, Backlane, and Cornmarket, close to Saint Audoen's, where the Geraghty family grew up. There was an array of guilds, for example for weavers, coopers, goldsmiths, shoe makers, tailors and bakers. Some other interesting guilds were tallow chandlers, soap boilers, brewers and malters, wax light makers and barber surgeons, the latter being responsible for the surviving use of the striped red and white barber's pole.

Prior to the arrival of Jim Larkin and James Connolly, the Irish trade union movement was highly fragmented with a multiplicity of small unions often pursuing the conflicting interests of their small elite membership. The crafts were usually better organised and had better recognition from employers than the labourers or general workers, who had in effect no strong organisation. The crafts were zealous about their status and maintained their influence and negotiating strength by protecting work standards and restricting the number of apprentices allowed into their trades.

The trades councils in Dublin, Belfast, Cork, Limerick and Drogheda brought some degree of common organisation to the cities, but were still mainly craft groupings. In 1894 they came together as the Irish Trade Union Congress (ITUC), based in the Trades Hall in Capel Street, Dublin. There were 119 delegates, only four of whom were women – two from Dublin and two from Belfast, representing small unskilled workers' unions. The majority came from British and Irish craft unions, so understandably the gathering was largely modelled on the British Trades Union Congress, the TUC.

When Larkin arrived in Ireland in 1907, he represented the British National Union of Dock Labourers (NUDL) and was involved in strikes in Belfast, Cork and Dublin. At the end of 1908, after disagreements within the NUDL, he set about founding his own union, the Irish Transport and General Workers' Union (ITGWU). Seán O'Casey, a great supporter of Larkin, described the beginning of the new union thus: 'In a room of a tenement in Townsend Street, with a candle in a bottle for a torch and a billy can of tea, with a few buns for a banquet, the church militant here on earth of the Irish workers, called the Irish Transport and General Workers Union, was founded, a tiny speck of flame now, but soon to become a pillar of fire.'

Townsend Street is in City Quay, very close to where both Tom and Lily Geraghty were born, in Asylum Yard, and where many of Dublin's coal heavers and dock workers lived. Lily's brothers, Jack and Andy O'Neill, were casual dockers who worked mainly on the coal boats and became early members of Larkin's new union.

Both Larkin and Connolly brought a syndicalist approach to trade union organisation, which was similar to the Industrial Workers of the World – the Wobblies – of Joe Hill in the United States. They placed the new union at the forefront of their socialist politics, espoused a direct action approach to workers' rights, encouraged greater solidarity, sympathy strikes, the blacklisting or boycotting of 'tainted goods' and put an emphasis on the organisation of the unskilled general workers. Their slogan, 'One Big Union', often resented by other unions, represented a major departure from the traditional craft- and grade-based trade unionism and gave a new dimension to the more conservative trade union movement. Their decision to create the Labour Party in 1912, a move forward from individuals carrying the labour stamp, helped to place the industrial labour movement at the heart of political ferment in the country in those critical years.

Larkin argued that 'I am an industrialist and at the same time appreciate the fact that labour can achieve a great deal through the intelligent use of the ballot. Why use one arm when we have two? Why not strike the enemy with both arms – the political and the economic?'

After the six-month lock-out of the ITGWU by William Martin Murphy and other Dublin employers in 1913, the Irish trade union movement was severely weakened. Although both Connolly and Larkin had vigorously opposed involvement in the 1914–1918 war, thousands of unemployed, victimised and demoralised Dublin workers had no option but to join the British Army to support their families. Sadly, many were killed or seriously injured in the unmerciful trench warfare of that conflict.

In spite of this enormous setback, the Irish Citizen Army, formed in November 1913 to defend the striking workers during the Lock-Out, continued to function. By the end of the Lock-Out it had only fifty members, but it continued to recruit and train and became a vital element of the Easter Rising in 1916. Seán O'Casey was the first secretary of the Citizen Army and helped to draft a new constitution, presented in March 1914 at a meeting chaired by Jim Larkin in Liberty Hall. When the Rising took place, James Connolly, acting general secretary of the ITGWU, was commander-in-chief of the republican forces and was to be executed for his part in the Rising.

The executions of James Connolly and Michael Mallon, followed shortly after by the death of William Partridge and the murder of Francis Sheehy-Skeffington, as well as the absence of Jim Larkin, who was in America, combined to leave a serious gap in the progressive leadership of the Irish labour movement.

Tom Johnson, Secretary of the ITUC, and Cathal O'Shannon made an impressive contribution to the progressive development of republican politics when they helped draft the historic Programme of the First Dáil, which was adopted in 1919. However, that programme was not seriously on the agenda of the conservative nationalist leaders in Sinn Féin, particularly those who took power after the 1921 Treaty.

Another great loss to the progressive development of political thinking came with the death of Liam Mellows, a prominent IRA leader executed by the Free State in December 1922. He had consistently espoused physical force as the means to secure the republic and had an aversion to politics. However, while he was jailed in Mountjoy in 1922, during the Civil War, he embraced many of Connolly's views about the character of any desired republic and recognised clearly, with Peadar O'Donnell and other prisoners, the need to combine both the political and social needs of the people in their struggle.

Perhaps one of the most damaging blows to the long-term role of labour and the trade union movement in Ireland was to come with the Larkin–O'Brien split of 1923. This was a trade union cold war, which divided the movement until William O'Brien retired in 1946 and Jim Larkin died in 1947.

Jim Larkin returned to Dublin in 1923 after serving three years of a ten-year sentence in Sing-Sing Prison for his political activities in the USA. Shortly after his return, differences arose with O'Brien and the executive council of the union. A bitter antagonism developed between Larkin and O'Brien, who had become general treasurer of the union in 1919. With rule changes and a more extensive organi-sation of rural branches, he had tightened his overall control of the organisation. Their differences were both political and personal and became so bitter that they resulted in two serious legal actions, one by Tom Foran (general president) and others against Larkin and one by Larkin against the ITGWU, Foran, O'Brien, Tom Kennedy and others in February 1924. These were extremely divisive and extended into complex disputes about the rules of the union, the property of Liberty Hall and 35 Parnell Square, and an injunction against Larkin entering the union premises. The courts generally found against Larkin, except on one question concerning two members of the union, who were paid officials and as such had no right to be members of the union's Execu-tive Council. The sordid details of these court actions were published by O'Brien and the ITGWU in a vindictive and personalised attack on the character of Jim Larkin, in a publication entitled 'The Attempt to Smash the Irish Transport and General Workers' Union'. Larkin, the titan of the Irish labour movement, was expelled and William O'Brien became general secretary.

When Peter Larkin, Jim Larkin's brother, founded the WUI in 1924, in the absence of Big Jim, who was in Moscow at a conference, two-thirds of the Dublin membership followed Larkin into the new union. Jim Larkin then became general secretary of the WUI.

The Civil War also created many divided loyalties, as did differ-ences about British- and Irish-based unions. The Labour Party, which was part of the ITUC, had 17 TDs elected in 1922 and sought to mediate between the pro- and anti-Treaty forces, with little success. They did oppose the Oath of Allegiance, but were also opposed to the republican rejection of the Treaty, and they entered the Free State Parliament. In the 1923 election they lost some support, but still elected 14 TDs.

The 1920s were bleak for workers, with high unemployment, low wages and little sympathy from the government of William Cosgrave. During the 1930s, under the Fianna Fáil government, supported by Labour and with pressure from the trade unions, some small progress was made on workers' rights. A Workmen's Compensation Act was introduced in 1934 and a Conditions of Employment Act in 1938, together with another Act governing conditions of employment in shops. An Agricultural Wages Board was set up in 1936; social welfare was improved and a widow's pension introduced.

These improvements generally resulted in increased support for Fianna Fáil among workers and did little to enhance the level of support for Labour. Over the years, politics in the twenty-six counties evolved into the 'two and a half-party system', reflecting the old Civil War divisions, with a 'half party' role for Labour and a large range of other smaller parties from time to time. One consistent feature of the larger parties, until recently, was a marked reluctance to challenge the religious control of education and health, or the dominance of charitable provision over national entitlement in areas such as poverty, children and social welfare.

In the North, the industrial labour movement has often had to cope with recurring outbreaks of sectarianism in the workplace. Protestant loyalism, the flipside of Catholic nationalism in the South, has been used over the decades to protect Unionist dominance by keeping the working class divided on sectarian grounds. That sectarianism was particularly virulent in 1920, when over seven thousand 'Catholics and bad Protestants' – 'bad' meaning those who had socialist sympathies or who disagreed with these purges – were expelled from the Belfast shipyards by Orange mobs.

Trade unions were well established in Northern Ireland because it was industrially developed earlier than the South, with a significant

level of union organisation in areas such as shipbuilding, general engineering, textiles, linen, tobacco and food. These unions were generally
amalgamated British craft unions, with the Amalgamated Transport
and General Workers' Union (ATGWU), part of the British Transport and General Workers' Union (T&G), being the largest general
workers' union. Many of the unions had a strong socialist or egalitarian
ethos and generally looked to the British Labour Party to address their
political concerns. From the foundation of the Northern State, unions
have also had to accept the divided loyalties of their members on the
national question, yet have worked hard to uphold the principles of
equal rights and equal standards for all their members. While some
political unity was forged in the early 1930s, violent sectarian attacks,
clearly stoked by extreme loyalist organisations, continued for short
periods, at least up to 1935.

In 1925, three trade union figures from very different backgrounds
had been elected as MPs in Belfast on behalf of the Northern Ireland
Labour party (NILP); Sam Kyle of the ATGWU, Billy McMullen of
the ITGWU and Jack Beattie of the blacksmiths' union. This trio were
extremely active in representing worker interests and gave workers a
united voice on many contentious legislative matters emanating from
London. That unity was frequently fractured in the following years
by political and sectarian conflict, yet the majority of trade union
members and their organisations sustained a belief in unity and co-operation on economic and social issues, including gender equality and
peace and civil rights issues.

After the reunification of the trade union movement in 1959, the
new structure of the Irish Congress of Trade Unions (ICTU), with a
specific Northern Ireland Committee, offered the hope of ongoing
unity and co-operation between the majority of trade unionists on the
island. After some initial differences about the home base of unions,
reasonable working arrangements were developed. A permanent office
in Belfast and a full-time Northern Ireland officer helped to maintain
a flexible approach to North–South relations; and the absence of any
obstacles to East–West participation by British-based unions created
a workable model which would be worthwhile for other organisations
to consider.

Members of trade unions in Dublin or Belfast or other parts of the country regularly participate in trade union conferences in London or Dublin and no one finds anything unusual about that. The Northern Ireland Committee (NIC) of Congress plays a valuable role in economic and industrial relations issues and deals constructively with representatives of the diverse political interests in Northern Ireland and also with UK government representatives. A policy of rotating the presidency of the ICTU between North and South at each conference has ensured that policy can be co-ordinated or differentiated to reflect the nature of the two economies.

For the Geraghty family, this structural evolution in the trade union movement saw Seán, the eldest, represent electricians in London's Fleet Street; Tom represented firemen and became an executive member of the WUI and SIPTU and developed very close relationships with fire fighters in Belfast, Glasgow, London, New York, and many other cities; and Sé, a branch secretary of the Amalgamated T&G in Waterford, had regular connections with officers in both Dublin and London. Des, as an industrial officer in the ITGWU and later president of SIPTU, and an Executive Council member of the ICTU, had multiple dealings with all unions, Irish and British, while Hugh, the youngest in the family, was Dublin district president of the Amalgamated Electrical Union (AEU), a British-based craft union, and later an industrial officer of the ICTU. None of them allowed themselves to be restricted by the national border down the Irish Sea, or allowed themselves to be constrained by the unnatural border between the North and the South of this country.

8

Burning of the Books

So they have set up a censorship of books in Ireland, and now at Irish ports, whose sole export is porter and men of genius, imported literature which is the product of Irish genius is seized and burned as dangerous contraband. And so tortured Ireland, which a few years ago asked for and received the sympathy of the world's intellectuals, now shows herself as a surly, sick bitch biting the hand that fed her.

- Liam O'Flaherty, 1932

Des was enjoying a leisurely read of *The Ragged-Trousered Philanthropists* in the small parlour room of their Drimnagh home. The book was written by Robert Tressell, who was actually a Dublin painter/signwriter named Robert Noonan. It is a wonderful read, a classic of socialist literature, which the author referred to as 'the story of twelve months in Hell, told by one of the damned', about the life of a casual house-painter in 'Mugsborough' – actually Hastings in Britain. It gives a powerful insight into the harsh world of drudgery for casual workers in the construction industry and is a more widely read and acclaimed case against crude, inhuman exploitation than any learned polemic on the subject.

Des's reading was rudely interrupted by the arrival of an unfamiliar Catholic priest at the front door of the house. Priests were not frequent visitors to their home, or indeed to most homes in the large sprawling working-class parish of Drimnagh. On the other hand, their door had been graced by many more unfamiliar characters over the years. This visitor was well turned out, young, clean-cut and excessively polite, asking Des, when he answered the door, if Mrs Geraghty was at home. Initially Des hesitated, as he knew his mother was busy in the tiny kitchenette preparing the family's evening meal. He also remembered that she was dressed in a less than flattering apron, covering an unfashionable top and rather soiled old skirt. He knew she was likely to be greatly embarrassed to receive this elegant visitor when she was in such sartorial disarray.

He was tempted for a brief moment to tell the priest that his mother wasn't at home, remembering an old city joke about the boy who told a rent collector 'me mammy says she isn't in'. But the formality of the priest made him suspect that the visit might be of some importance, requiring the presence of his mother. He also knew that recently there had been some unfavourable attention drawn to the family in the media, as Seán, his eldest brother, along with some other young men from the Drimnagh area, had been arrested for involvement in the 1956 IRA border campaign. This news had drawn a hostile public response from the local parish priest, with a stern warning to parents about the sinful nature of these activities, in Mourne Road Church at Sunday morning Mass. His father, Tom, normally a quietly spoken and regular Mass attender, was present in the church. Incensed by the hostile tone of the sermon, he stood up and walked out, saying loudly as he left: 'You and the bishops said the same thing about the Fenians and the Volunteers.'

Then again, perhaps this visit could be about more mundane matters, such as the church collection or other routine parish affairs. Des told Lily about the clerical visitor at the door who had specifically asked for her. As expected, she asked him to usher the priest into the front room and keep him occupied while she washed her hands and face and got rid of her scruffy apron and top. For the few minutes the reverend gentleman had to wait, he managed to carry out a detailed inspection of the large collection of books and records packed into the shelves around the walls of the small front room. This parlour was a kind of Aladdin's cave of miscellaneous printed material, which served both as a library and quiet rest room for the family.

There was a great variety of books there, by such authors as Patrick McGill, Jack London, James Connolly, Maud Gonne, Karl Marx, Padraig Pearse, Emily Lawless, W.B. Yeats, Peadar O'Donnell, Lady Gregory, Seán O'Casey, Vladimir Lenin, Antonio Gramsci, Dean Swift, Alice Milligan, Maria Edgeworth, Shakespeare, Wordsworth, Robbie Burns, Joe Tomelty, George Russell (AE), John Millington Synge, and even Sir Robert Baden-Powell. There was also a whole series of Free Thinker Library books and a wide collection of pamphlets, papers and periodicals. All five of the boys, as well as their father and mother, were voracious readers. Like most people at that time, they had no television and therefore this room was also a place of entertainment, often an impromptu music room, with a wind-up gramophone and a large collection of old 78 records. These included recordings of artists such as John McCormack, Paul Robeson, Percy French, the Kilfenora Céilí Band, the fiddler Michael Coleman and Robert Emmet's 'Speech from the Dock'. There was a disc of Constance Markievicz's 'Battle Hymn' and other miscellaneous tracks. There was also an old crackly radio set, which provided occasional entertainment for friends and visitors without interfering with the rest of the family, who normally occupied the rear kitchen-cum-dining room at the back of the house. It was the only available room in which to entertain a visitor.

When Lily appeared in the front room she apologised for the delay, explaining that she had been in the process of preparing dinner, but assuring the priest that he was very welcome. Without formally intro-ducing himself, apparently assuming that his prominent white collar was sufficient introduction, he asked, 'Mrs Geraghty, who is reading all these books?'

Lily said, 'Sure everyone in this house loves reading and they keep adding to the collection, although we are running out of shelf space to accommodate all the books.'

'But Mrs Geraghty', he replied sharply, 'are you aware that there are a lot of banned books here, that are not suitable reading for young impressionable minds?'

'Sure Father, I keep a close eye on all these books and I can assure you there is nothing indecent or obscene here; and the lads are well able to make up their own minds about what books they read. I'm always pleased to see them reading — and aren't they better reading books here than getting into all kinds of trouble out on the streets?'

Des could see the colour rising in his mother's cheeks, knowing how important reading was in her life and the huge value she placed on good literature. Having had little formal education, she depended on books and newspapers for access to knowledge and learning; and she had ever since childhood. She had often facilitated special customers by importing books not available in Ireland and providing them along with the newspaper delivery.

The uninvited priest, who had as yet failed to inform her who he was, or why he was there, appeared to have assumed some divine right to criticise her about her family's reading habits. His rather censorious and unfriendly remarks had clearly irritated Des's mother and had made him unwelcome in her house.

'Father', she said, 'I don't know who you are, or why you called, but I think you might be in the wrong house. I'm sure you could be better engaged spending your time with some other parishioners, who might want your advice on more important things than reading. So can I say goodbye to you now; and God Bless, Father.'

This put an abrupt end to any further conversation and it was left to young Des to escort a very uncomfortable young cleric to the front door.

This visitor would not have been aware that censorship was a very sensitive subject in the house, as a number of banned Irish authors were well known to both Lily and Tom, as well as other members of the household. No one in the family had ever seen a full list of banned books, but they did know how often some books were inaccessible and how censorship, both official and unofficial, was exercised. They knew that in many cases it was to the detriment of decent writers and those with leftist or liberal opinions. It also deprived the general public of access to national and international opinions disapproved of by the philistines of the Irish establishment.

The publicly proclaimed reason for the introduction of the 1929 Censorship of Publications Act was to protect the Irish people from 'indecent or obscene literature, exposure to crime, or material which advocated the unnatural prevention of conception'. However, since its introduction, it had been become much more widely used as a sectarian device to support conservatism in the State. It was, unfortunately, manipulated by people afraid of any new ideas that might challenge the views of a deeply entrenched Church and State establishment.

From 1929 to 1946, there was absolutely no recourse for writers to any right of appeal against the censorship of their works – banned by a faceless, five-member group appointed by the Minister for Justice. This created bitterness and alienation among authors, many of whom responded with self-imposed exile. Ironically, they often found a safer haven in Britain, the land of the historic oppressor. Others, like Joyce and Beckett, found more distant pastures where their creative writing was greatly celebrated.

In 1946, an Act was passed that allowed an Appeals Board to be instituted by the Minister if five members of the Oireachtas sought it. Later, in 1967, further changes were made which limited the period for which a book could be banned to twelve years, but again provided that a book could be re-banned, if resubmitted to the censorship board.

Perhaps one of the saddest and most sinister consequences of this literary fascism was visited on an old couple living a quiet, modest and peaceful life, far from the consciousness of any of the authorities in Dublin. In 1942, *The Tailor and Ansty*, an anthropological book by Eric Cross, an English scientist, about the life of this rural couple in County Kerry, was banned because of its 'bawdy humour'. Frank O'Connor, one of our finest short story writers, wrote that only one public figure, Sir John Keane, defended it in Seanad Éireann. He pointed out that:

One of our national heroes described the Tailor as 'a dirty old man,' and his wife 'a morán'. As a result, that kind old couple who had offered hospitality to students from all over Ireland were boycotted. I am not exaggerating. I was there with them one night when a branch of a tree was driven between the wall and the latch so that we were imprisoned. Three priests appeared at their little cottage and forced that dying old man to go on his knees at his own hearth and burn the only copy he had of his own book.

He went on to point out that in 1946, when Justice Haugh took over the Censorship Appeal Board, he had concluded that *The Tailor and Ansty* was not obscene in any way. At that stage the poor Tailor was dead and the book was out of print. Subsequently the book was taught in Harvard University by an American anthropologist, and a statue of the Tailor stands, in defiance of the philistines in Ireland, as one of the Apostles over a Catholic church in San Francisco.

Many writers of banned books were stigmatised and regarded as legitimate targets for harassment by religious zealots. Even writers who were not banned were treated as suspect and books with any reference to sexual matters were removed from libraries. Sales and distribution were discouraged by regular visits to booksellers by religious activists such as members of the Catholic Truth Society.

Others managed to ridicule the legislation and availed of its notoriety to increase the demand for their publications. Many years later, Des was to hear Brendan Behan singing out boldly, for all to hear, in the Bailey public house on Duke Street:

Oh me name is Brendan Behan, I'm the leader of the banned,
Although we're few in number we're the best band in the land
We're read at wakes and weddings and in every parish hall,
and under library counters, sure you'll have no trouble at all.

Why wouldn't Brendan Behan, never one to miss an opportunity to shock his audience, not sing about his 'honourable association' with such luminaries of international literature as Samuel Beckett, Ernest Hemingway, Sinclair Lewis, Kate O'Brien, James Baldwin, Saul Bellow, H.G. Wells, Marcel Proust, Arthur Koestler, Dylan Thomas, Jean-Paul Sartre, Alberto Moravia, Christina Stead, Nadine Gordimer, Christopher Isherwood and other major literary figures of the century, all of whom had had their works banned by the Irish Censorship Board?

This experience of seeing so many valuable books banned prompted Frank O'Connor to declare that 'Irish censorship is an insult to Irish intelligence … if you feel otherwise I can only say that Irish intelligence is a contradiction in terms.'

It was our home-grown Irish writers who suffered the most. The stigma of being banned often had consequences far beyond the literary sphere. It affected them in their families, communities and often in their jobs. John McGahern, a modest and decent gentlemen, did not enjoy the notoriety associated with the banning of his book *The Dark*. He said that 'one has a family in Ireland and it was quite a social disgrace.' He lost his job as a teacher and was not defended by his union, the Irish National Teachers' Organisation (INTO), which sought to justify this failure by using a technicality about the status of his membership. One man, at a meeting with his union, said: 'McGahern, what entered your head to go and marry a foreign woman when there's hundreds of thousands of Irish women going around with their tongues hanging out for a husband?' McGahern was amused by the 'tongues hanging out', as he had never seen any women acting in that fashion. He had also been informed, privately, that John Charles McQuaid, the Archbishop of Dublin and a mighty power in the land, had indicated that he would not support the union in pay negotiations with the government if they backed McGahern in his fight against his dismissal.

Edna O'Brien, from County Clare, who emigrated to Britain in the 1960s, said that her family felt very ashamed when, in her twenties, her first book was banned. She said that when the second book came out, one woman said: 'We're beginning to think that the first book was a prayer book by comparison.' Another woman who read it reputedly claimed to be ill and felt she was possessed by the Devil, so the priest had to visit her house. This was followed by copies of O'Brien's book being burned in the chapel grounds.

Brinsley MacNamara was a victim of a similar form of unofficial censorship when he wrote *The Valley of the Squinting Windows*. He lived in the small town of Delvin in County Meath, and many of the citizens of that town thought they were in the book. This led to great conflict and consternation in the town. His father was actually assaulted; and on one Saturday evening, when there was fighting up and down the street about the publication, a local butcher burned the book and one old lady was reported to remark, 'Thanks be to God the trouble is over now, the book is burned.'

Serious opposition to this repression of intellectual endeavour had begun with Oliver St John Gogarty's opposition to literary censorship in the Seanad in 1929. He feared we would become a nation of fanatics and we would 'make use of our recent liberty to fill every village and hamlet with literary pimps'. AE – George Russell – also published a number of well-argued philosophical views against censorship, including this:

If people could be made virtuous by an Act of Parliament, we would submit to whatever restrictions might be imposed. But we do not believe that evidence can be brought that anywhere censorship over publications have been successful in their objects, and they have always been ridiculous.

In 1927, the Council of Irish Bishops in Maynooth had solemnly warned the public that:

The evil one is ever setting his snares for unwary feet. At the moment, his traps for the innocent are chiefly the dance hall, the bad book, the indecent paper, the motion picture, the immodest fashion in female dress, all of which tend to destroy the virtuous characteristics of our race.

This rhetoric encouraged a view that by purging all indecencies and foreign influences we could make Ireland a spiritual model for the world. Seán O'Casey, in a note of sarcasm, wrote in one of his auto-biographies, 'the priests will drag the people of Ireland into heaven by the scruff of their necks.'

George Bernard Shaw, T.S. Eliot, W.B. Yeats, Liam O'Flaherty and AE were the most virulent opponents of the 1929 Act, but they were joined by many others at home and abroad over the years. In the 1940s, Seán Ó Faoláin, Frank O'Connor and Peadar O'Donnell became prom-inent opponents of censorship. The anti-censorship campaigning was done mainly on the pages of *The Bell* and through frequent letters to newspapers such as the *Irish Times*. Northern writers such as Ben Kiely, Brian Moore, Sam Thompson and Maurice Leitch were also active opponents of the legislation. Leitch, a Northern Protestant, claimed he was totally alienated from the literary tradition of the Republic and could see little difference between the repressive ideologies of the two states.

Over the years, Des had grown increasingly resentful of this national isolationism and the authoritarianism of the bishops of the Catholic Church. He knew and valued many dedicated religious priests, nuns and brothers who gave their whole lives to education, charity, welfare and human rights. His parents spoke lovingly of Father Albert and Father Dominic of the Capuchin Order and the Little Sisters of Whitefriar Street, who quietly laid out and washed the dead. He was also a good friend of Father Austin Flannery and a few more clerics, but he found these tended to be more the exception than the rule.

In more recent years, he recognised the true Christianity of clerics like Brother Kevin, Father Peter McVerry and Sister Stanislaus, all concerned with the poor and needy, and viewed them as national treasures. He also knew and respected the intellectual independence and activism of Sister Benvenuta and also had a high regard for the former Archbishop of Dublin, Diarmuid Martin. However, he felt that an unholy and unhealthy alliance still existed between Church and State in the Republic. He was disappointed that this was presided over, for many years, by such a national figure as the Taoiseach, and later President, Éamon de Valera, along with the Archbishop of Dublin, John Charles McQuaid. In practice he believed that this alliance had lot more to do with temporal interests than with any genuine spirituality.

He remembered how at school in the 1950s copies of banned books were often secretly circulated under the desks. Edna O'Brien's novels about women and love were very popular and widely available in the 1960s, especially in Dublin bookshops. The adventures and sexual exploits of Lee Dunne's characters became a favourite choice of rebellious teenagers in the 1970s. He felt this was a not unexpected consequence of the ill-judged policies of an insecure and insular state. It arose from the clearly mistaken belief that all foreign and 'corrupting' influences could be kept at bay by threats, fear, diktat or suppression.

9

Down in the Dark
Are the Tunnel Tigers

On a wet and windy Friday evening in June 1959, Des stood on the deck of the mail boat in Dún Laoghaire, en route for London. After much negotiation with his parents, as he was only fifteen years of age, he had persuaded them to let him make the journey to London to see his brothers Seán and Tom, who were both working there. He also hoped to earn some decent money for himself to meet his needs later on in the year.

Every summer holiday from school, Des had secured some small employment to improve the family income and also to earn enough for himself to pay for camping and hiking activities for the rest of the year. Since losing his first regular job as a dairy boy in the Liberties, in his early teens, when the family were exiled to Drimnagh, Des had a series of interesting employment experiences. These ranged from boiling live lobsters and delivering filleted fish and chickens for Johnny Lennox in the Iveagh Market or from his shop in Francis Street, to selling petrol and oil in the Broadstone filling station and cutting massive garden hedges, with hand shears, for a doctor in Terenure who worked in the Drimnagh Clinic. However, he had been sacked from his lowly petrol station job when he looked for a day off, or payment in lieu, for working the August bank holiday. That was an early lesson for Des on the hazards of having to negotiate with an uncooperative employer without any trade union backing.

Des was surprised at how packed the British Rail ship was – men, women and children, mostly poorly dressed, carrying a great variety of shabby leather travel cases, bags, baggage and some with a solid supply of bottled Guinness. He was pleased to see an elderly man, obviously from the west of Ireland, playing an old melodeon for a group of friends and family tucked into a corner of the deck. They were speaking in Irish and appeared to be a warm and friendly group with whom to travel. He decided to keep close to this group for the journey as he loved the music and reckoned they would make good travelling companions. He was not mistaken in that judgment, as they welcomed him readily into their company.

His observation of the other passengers on board was interrupted by the arrival of very attractive young woman, with a file in her hand and wearing an identity label, enquiring about his destination. He was initially reluctant to disclose any personal information to this complete stranger, but relaxed when she informed him that she was a member of the Legion of Mary and was on board before the ship sailed to give advice to people emigrating to Britain. She asked him if he was aware of the Irish Centre on Camden Square and suggested that he make contact with the priests in the parish church nearest his living quarters in London. After a brief and generally friendly conversation, she departed abruptly when he asked her, tongue in cheek, if she might consider going to London herself, as he would be delighted to meet her there.

That journey gave Des a valuable insight into the shabby treatment doled out to Irish emigrants, who were pouring out of the country like an unstoppable river all through the 1950s and 1960s. The conditions for most ordinary passengers on the ships, who did not have cabins, were miserable; and when the weather worsened that night, many people became violently sea-sick on the deck. The majority had to suffer without adequate facilities for food or rest. The few available toilets were stuffed with paper and poorly maintained.

One could not help feeling that the Irish emigrants were being treated no better than the live cattle below deck on the Liverpool route, with whom they shared their journeys when crossing the Irish Sea. They were packed too tightly on over-crowded ships that were poorly serviced and lacked any decent facilities. The train journey from Holyhead to London was little better, as many young people, especially the men, stood drinking all night in the corridors of the train, to allow the women, children and elders avail of the limited compartment seating that was available.

The early morning arrival on the cold platform of Euston station provided other interesting revelations. The Legion of Mary insignia was very visible at the station and many Irish relatives and friends were also there to welcome newly arrived travellers. On leaving the train, though, it was obvious that there were also quite a number of unsavoury characters around, approaching young single passengers, male or female, and making propositions of various kinds to the new arrivals. Since Des had to wait at the station – Tom had been delayed for a short while on his way to meet him – he had several approaches from these people, asking him for smokes, offering him lifts, suggesting employment opportunities and looking for very personal information.

Being a bit of a Dublin street gurrier, Des refused to engage with any of these opportunists and left the station platform to wait outside for Tom at the entrance. There he was surprised to see so many rough sleepers outside the station. He then realised that the Legion of Mary presence might be a more valuable safeguard for lonely emigrant arrivals than he had first thought. It became evident to him that people coming with no pre-arranged place to live or work, in this vast and overwhelming city, could well be at serious risk and might certainly need some care and support.

Tom shared a single, reasonably large room with two double beds with Phil Clarke and two other Dubliners. This was in Highbury, near the Arsenal football stadium. One of the other occupants of the room was Rory Cowan, son of Peadar Cowan, a well-known Irish politician. Rory was later to be father to another Rory, of more recent *Mrs Brown's Boys* fame. Curiously enough, Rory Senior was at that time a barman in Mooney's on the Strand in London, while also a sitting councillor on Dublin Corporation. He proved to be an invaluable asset for Des by furnishing him with an impressive character reference, which helped him secure his first job as an office boy in a small hardware establishment near The Angel in London.

The house near Arsenal was owned by an Irish landlady, a decent woman, warm and welcoming towards all the latest Irish arrivals. The house was in Highbury, near Finsbury Park, the Seven Sisters Road and Holloway Road, where a large population of Irish people had settled. There was also a large population of Greek Cypriots in that area, along with a multiplicity of other nationalities. It would be hard to assess how many actual Londoners lived there, as there were so many different nationalities. So it seemed that it would not be difficult to live and work in London without ever knowing any English people.

That summer and the three following summers, Des stayed with Tom while he worked in London. Later, in the 1960s, he was employed in Gravesend, on the Thames, having been sent there on behalf of a Dublin-based telecoms contractor named Dictograph. Every day on that stint, rather than staying in Gravesend, he preferred the very early start in Finsbury Park, an underground journey on the Victoria line, followed by a further series of underground hops until he was picked up by a fellow worker for the final few miles' drive into Gravesend. The journey, approximately thirty miles, was only made possible by the efficient underground system. He couldn't but feel thankful to the thousands of underground workers who had worked so hard to make that daily journey possible, for he never wished to stay overnight in Gravesend, so far down the River Thames and so far away from his friends in north London.

Des enjoyed his time in London, mainly because he always knew his stay was a temporary one. It was a good time and place for having new experiences in a thriving, international and multi-racial city. Unfortunately, his enjoyment was not shared by many of the Irish people he met, who realised that they had little prospect of ever returning home. They worked and made the most of their adopted home, and over time, some succeeded in substantially improving their living standards. Those emigrants often told Des that they liked London but missed their friends and families left behind in Ireland. He found the many Irish pubs and dance halls in London that were the usual gathering-places for recent arrivals. They were attracted by the lively ambience of these establishments, often helped by the familiarity of the Irish music, and the opportunity they gave them to meet other people from home.

It was his time in London that gave Des an interesting insight into the true nature of Irish society, which many in the Irish establishment at home could blissfully ignore. There was no 'digging for gold on the streets', and many emigrants experienced a difficult and lonely exist-ence without family support around them. They sent money home but often lived themselves in sub-standard accommodation. This was seen as part of their assumed 'temporary' existence in Britain. However, it was evident from the number of older and down-at-heel Irish people on the streets of London that, for many, their temporary status had become more of a permanent nightmare. Des felt that Christy Moore's song captured that experience very succinctly:

Oh, I'm missing you, I'd give all for the price of a flight,
Oh I'm missing you, under Piccadilly's neon lights.

Des found that Irish music was popular in particular pubs around Camden Town. There was even an Irish language choir, based in a house at 123 Camden Road, called Cumann Ceol Bhinn, the 'group of sweet music'. This choir was run by the O'Boyle family, originally from Donegal, who had a great love of the Irish music and language and participated in regular choral competitions. The father, Dr O'Boyle, was a great favourite of his Irish patients, and his wife, together with their daughter Maura, created a very merry, home-from-home atmos-phere there for the members of the choir. In the O'Boyle house, after the formal choir practices were over, the craic would be mighty. Tom Geraghty met his lovely future wife, Mairéad, there; she was a loyal member of the choir and a native of Ballyduff, in west Waterford.

Des was well aware that the high rates of unemployment and emigration were attributable to the many serious economic problems in the young Irish state. However, he was surprised to discover that many young Irish people he met told him they had left the country, and often a job, to escape from repressive aspects of Irish society. Women often complained of the unpleasant control and guilt constantly visited on them at home.

Another surprise, for Des, was the number of native Irish speakers he met on building sites, or around Camden Town, or in the London Irish dance halls, or the huge sawdust-floored pub in Finsbury Park during the building of the Victoria Line, which began in 1959 and continued during the 1960s. It seemed to him that the Irish language and Gaelic culture were living in exile, on the streets of London, while their recent loss was being lamented daily in the homes of Connemara, Mayo, Donegal and Kerry. The large pub in Finsbury Park was opposite the railway station and was a regular meeting-place for the 'tunnel tigers', the underground miners on the Victoria Project, after their eight-hour-plus shifts underground. Des saw a number of violent eruptions and fights in that pub at weekends after excessive drink had been consumed. One Connemara friend explained to him that some of these outbursts were a direct result of the 'bends' – too many underground workers were not taking the full hour and a half decompression time in a steel chamber before heading to the pub for their drinks. After an eight-hour stint in the dark, miserable underground, many would be impatient with this slow procedure. They would head for the pub immediately for a few pints, but could pay dearly later for their undue haste, with unpredictable bouts of madness and pain.

These underground workers, many of whom were Irish, carried an identity tag to inform any ambulance or medical personnel that they needed more decompression time to recover. Forty-three deaths were officially recorded, of people of different nationalities, on the construction of that Victoria Line project, along with another seventy-four serious injuries. These were the officially recorded casualties, but many believed that the number of minor injuries underground, or the consequent but later deaths and injuries above ground, were never fully calculated. Dominic Behan captured many of these experiences very well in his evocative and humorous song of that period, 'Building Up and Tearing Old England Down'.

Des himself worked on a number of different construction sites in London as an electrician's mate, a category not so common in Ireland but quite common in the British construction industry. His jobs entailed dealing with heavy tools and electrical equipment, fixing cables, connection boxes and metal trunking, moving or placing ladders; and a variety of the other odd jobs required by electricians working under pressure on a building site.

A particularly happy and interesting period for Des was when he was working on the construction of the John Lewis store on Oxford Street, in the fashionable West End of London. His regular electrical workmate was a Greek Cypriot and former EOKA prisoner, who was very informative about EOKA's struggle for Cypriot independence from Britain and how the old 'divide and conquer' approach was cynically used to keep the Greek and Turkish communities on the island apart.

Some of the work on that site was on the front of the building and this afforded Des and his mate a wonderful view of Oxford Street below, with its many buses, cars and pedestrians – some of the best-dressed and most attractive denizens of the trendy West End. There was also a fantastic group of street jazz musicians, who paraded up and down regularly, entertaining all and sundry in the warm summer sunshine. An additional bonus on that site was the proximity of Hyde Park, where every shade of opinion from the sublime to the ridiculous could be heard from the speakers at Hyde Park Corner. Des spent many lunch breaks and weekends there, learning about complex conflicts in such distant places as Africa, the Far East, Vietnam, the Philippines or the Caribbean.

The Irish tricolour and Starry Plough were also regularly exhibited there in Hyde Park, by groups such as the Connolly Association. A character named McGuinness, a one-time unemployed activist in Dublin, was one of the most entertaining speakers. He would end his comical diatribe by telling his audience, 'I can't ask you for money, but if you put it in my pocket I won't be a bit offended.' His other declaration was that he owed more than six months' rent but didn't worry about it because his landlady was worried and he saw no point in two people worrying about the same problem.

Another great speaker in Hyde Park was a Mayo man named Durcan who often spoke on behalf of the British Communist Party. When seeking to recruit new members to his cause, he would frequently outline the horrible imprisonment, torture, persecution and death of his comrades in many parts of the globe. One sceptical English listener turned to Des after listening to Durcan's fervent plea for people to join the party and said, 'Imagine asking anyone to join an outfit like that!'

Des also spent some time working for an electrical contractor on the building of the National Heart Hospital, close to Harley Street in the West End. He had a very serious accident on that site when he was caught under the freely descending platform of a hoist. This was for carrying cement, sand, building blocks or wheelbarrows, etc., up to various levels of the building. Des was busy mixing sand and cement from a sand pile where the water hose was strapped to the bottom of the hoist, when someone, without warning, released the hoist from a floor above. He was struck by the heavy platform of the hoist on the head, shoulders and body, and was trapped under its full weight. Two lucky factors probably saved Des's life. One was the sand pile, which created a relatively soft landing. The other was a spring mechanism on the hoist itself, which stopped it about a foot from the ground before it started descending more slowly to the bottom. He was flattened to the ground and trapped in the twelve inches of space in the sand under the hoist. A number of workers immediately rushed in and lifted the platform just high enough for Des to be slowly dragged out. An emergency ambulance arrived soon after and took him to the Emergency Department of University College Hospital. He had some minor head injuries and scars front and back, a broken ankle and multiple cuts and bruises to his legs and body, but the most serious injury was a cracked spine. That particular one kept him in hospital for the best part of a month. He was told afterwards that he had had a remarkable recovery and that his youthful physique had helped a lot in his pace of recovery from the spinal damage.

Des's unplanned hospital sojourn proved to be a valuable opportunity for him to catch up on some solid reading, which might otherwise have been unlikely in his teens. He tackled, among other books, *War and Peace*, Seán O'Casey's autobiographies, *Ulysses*, Marx and Engels on Ireland, *Red Star Over China*, *Borstal Boy* and the complete works of Oscar Wilde. After that spell in hospital, Des returned to Ireland and did not go back to London to work until about seven years later.

Some years earlier, on the Easter weekend of 1959, Tom, Seán and a large contingent of Irish workers had joined the historic Aldermaston March for its return leg to London as part of the Ban the Bomb protests by the Campaign for Nuclear Disarmament (CND). That year, about 60,000 people participated in the event and by 1961 it had grown to 150,000. It set the scene for the growth of the whole radical youth culture of the early 1960s. The young people's movement of the 1960s was generally associated with an anti-establishment awareness, and the Ban the Bomb logo became the universal symbol of peace and disarmament, appearing on walls, posters, T-shirts and as a backdrop to concerts and even festivals, such as Glastonbury.

An Irish branch of the CND was formed in Dublin by John de Courcy Ireland, supported by Peadar O'Donnell, Owen Sheehy-Skeffington and Hubert Butler. Luke Kelly, with the Dubliners, helped to popularise two of the great anti-nuclear songs of the time – 'The Sun is Burning in the Sky' and 'The Button Pusher' – which Luke and his brother Jimmy sang with great gusto at many venues over the years.

That peace theme has continued to mobilise people in many parts of the world and although it could be argued that it has not had much success anywhere, it did create an awareness of how vulnerable humanity is to a nuclear catastrophe. It also led to the Nuclear Non-Proliferation Treaty talks, which opened in 1968. The treaty was ratified in 1970 and subsequently signed by 191 states, including the major nuclear powers. It's also interesting that campaigns such as Greenpeace, from 1992 onwards, the Greenham Common Women's Peace Camp of 1981–83, and their later peace camps, all grew out of the Ban the Bomb movement of the 1960s.

It was also this movement which linked young people in the United States, Britain, Ireland and Scotland in the folk music revival of the 1960s. The major figure in that revival was undoubtedly Ewan MacColl in Britain, who was well complemented by Pete Seeger and Joan Baez in the USA. They drew inspiration from the music and songs of earlier radicals such as Paul Robeson, Woody Guthrie, and the Wobblies (Industrial Workers of the World) songsters such as Joe Hill, Ralph Chaplin and T-Bone Slim.

The 'Bread and Roses' theme from the 1912 poem of James Oppenheim helped to rally and bring together the women's movement and the international labour movements. The most successful international singer of that US revival was undoubtedly Bob Dylan, a great composer and performer whose songs are still sung all around the world. Folk music clubs cropped up all over England, Wales and Scotland with a fusion of diverse national and international themes and performers. Social experiences and a myriad of progressive causes were shared with the more traditional themes of love, hate or rebellion in these generally left-of-centre venues.

Des attended a number of singing sessions and concerts organised by the Young Socialists, as well as Scottish and Irish events where the songs of Robbie Burns and Ewan MacColl, Dominic Behan, Pete Seeger, Bob Dylan, Bob Marley and Joan Baez were performed. Irish and Scottish music was always welcomed. In the folk clubs, Des found that there was always a genuine respect shown to performers, which was not always so evident in the noisy public houses. Irish and Scottish performers found a new home in these English venues, where their natural affinity with folk and traditional themes was greatly appreciated. Frank Harte, in his 1978 introduction to *Songs of Dublin*, pointed out, correctly, that 'While people discuss at length the folksong revival in England and America at the present time and the ethnomusicologists wax eloquently on its various aspects, we in this country have been spared the sacredness of a revival due to the fact that the tradition of singing songs has never died.'

In 1958, a serious bout of racism had erupted in Notting Hill, leading to major violence in that part of London. After the 1939–45 war, many African-Caribbean people had migrated to Britain and a substantial number of them had settled in the general area of Notting Hill. A number of minor incidents, in which rival groups of white and black people confronted each other, escalated into a much more systemic racist attack on the black communities there. This was encouraged by Sir Oswald Mosley's Union Movement, which was advocating the repatriation of Caribbean immigrants. Other aggressive groups emerged, such as the White Defence League, the Keep Britain White group and white teddy boys, who conducted regular attacks on young black people in that area. Increasingly, the black population became better organised and fought back. A number of serious confrontations resulted, which culminated in a major court case where one judge imposed jail sentences of five years and fines of £500 on 72 white and 36 black participants.

Arising from these violent racist confrontations, there was a more widespread mobilisation of anti-fascist groups on the left, including many Irish workers who were opposed to such fascist-inspired racist attacks on migrants. A Trinidad and Tobago journalist named Claudia Jones, together with Rhaune Laslett, organised a Solidarity Caribbean Carnival in St Pancras Town Hall to counteract the racist violence and to utilise their great music and culture to encourage greater support for the beleaguered Caribbean people in London. The event was a resounding success and led to the remarkable annual Notting Hill Carnival, which has been a major cultural event in London ever since. Held in the Kensington area over two days each year, on the August bank holiday weekend, it is now considered Europe's biggest street party and has been known to attract up to two and a half million people and to have forty thousand volunteers involved, as well as nine thousand police. It's a stunning example of how sharing a people's music can not only entertain but also contribute to developing a better appreciation of other aspects of their way of life, such as cuisine, dance, dress, art and language. The performance of their own music and song helped to instil a self-confidence and pride among these black Caribbean people who would otherwise have felt totally isolated and rejected in their adopted country. Who hasn't heard and been moved by the pounding beat and strong lyrics of Bob Marley's 'Stand Up for Your Rights'?

Each day Des travelled on the Victoria line underground across the city of London, he couldn't help but remember, with a mixture of both pride and sadness, the unwritten stories of all those migrant workers who made that remarkable journey possible. It was their painstaking and dangerous tunnelling job under the city that inspired Ewan MacColl to write those emotional lines in the song 'The Tunnel Tigers' to record the blood, sweat and tears of the thousands of Irish workers who made that tunnel possible.

Down in the dark are the Tunnel Tigers
Far from the sun and the light of day.
Down in the land that the sea once buried
They're driving a tunnel through the London clay.
Up with the shield and jack it! Ram it!
Driving a tunnel through the London clay.

10

Police Dogs and City Bowsies

On a cold October night in 1962, Des Geraghty and his friend Davy Pickett from Drimnagh were distributing a newsletter called *Forward* for the National Progressive Democrats (NPD), a small party led by Dr Noël Browne TD and Jack McQuillan TD. For many years, since he entered politics in 1948, Noël Browne had been an active campaigner for radical reform of the healthcare and welfare services. His passionate desire for reform had placed him in almost continuous battles with both Church and State, as well as with most of the established political parties. He is best known for his patient-centred Mother and Child Scheme of 1948, which drew the wrath of the Catholic hierarchy and elite elements of the medical profession.

In the Ireland of the forties, a country with very poor medical facilities and primitive levels of care for both mothers and their children, Browne's proposals for a no-means-test service were considered an outrageous attack on the authority of the Catholic Church and a sinister communist threat to the State. After years of gruelling combat with all the establishment interests in Irish society, protected by the fear and caution of so many existing political parties, the small NPD party appeared to these two young campaigners of the early 1960s the only serious prospect for radical change.

On that dark October night, Des and Davy were unaware of the ominous threat of a USA–USSR nuclear war over the Cuban Missile

Crisis, which had erupted when the USA discovered that Cuba was installing Russian missiles as part of its new defence system. When the two friends entered a long narrow pub on the north side of Dublin, all eyes were focused on a small television behind the bar. A BBC newsreader was reporting on the crisis. When US President John F. Kennedy appeared, speaking in a vigorous and determined fashion, the whole pub erupted in a loud burst of applause. When the bearded Cuban President Fidel Castro followed him on screen, Des and Davy both applauded, to the obvious annoyance of the local clientele. For Davy and Des, Fidel Castro was the heroic revolutionary leader who had defeated the army of the dictator Batista and expelled his financiers and Mafia associates, who had turned the whole island of Cuba into a land of gambling casinos and an extensive brothel for rich Americans. Castro had set about a radical transformation of Cuban society and in the previous year, 1961, his small army had routed a large CIA-backed military invasion of mercenaries led by members of the previous administration at the Bay of Pigs.

However, the potential consequences of a nuclear war were far from the thoughts of that public house gathering, who only saw two trouble-makers supporting a wild bearded foreigner, bellowing in Spanish and threatening their beloved Irish hero, President John F. Kennedy. Two of them turned abruptly from their drinks at the bar and pinned Davy Pickett against the back wall of the pub. They proceeded to beat him viciously about the head and face. Seeing what was happening, Des rushed from the other end of the bar to the defence of his friend, only to be intercepted by another group with vicious kicks and smacks to his head and body. Des and Davy were saved from major injuries by the narrowness of the pub, which did not allow enough space for more than two attackers at any time. However, they managed to smash Davy's glasses and stamp on the frames when they fell on the floor. Davy was a gentle intellectual type and he was shocked by this unexpected attack. He had never assaulted anyone in his life, so it took a lot of kicking, arm-swinging and dragging by Des to clear enough space for a rapid and undignified retreat out of the door. Outside, Des's dazed and blinded friend had to be hurried protesting down the street, for fear that the gang in the pub might mount a follow-up attack, which could have been even worse.

On the other side of the city, on the night of the 23 October, an open meeting of the NPD took place in its basement meeting-room on Kildare Street. There was a general sense of foreboding at the meeting; people were only too aware of the possible consequences of a nuclear holocaust if the US military launched its threatened attack on the Russian-installed defence missiles in Cuba. While attendees were discussing some more mundane political issues, the chairman John Byrne pointed out the futility of their deliberations if the international crisis could result in 'a no tomorrow for anyone'. He suggested that they take to the streets to demonstrate their deep concern about what might happen and try to raise public awareness of the threat that was hanging over humanity at that critical time.

A small band of supporters were quickly assembled and, led by party leader Noël Browne, set out on an orderly walk up Kildare Street to Stephen's Green, down Grafton Street and along Nassau Street, with the intention of walking to the American Embassy to hand in a message of protest. The protesters were joined en route by some small groups of good-natured young people and students who decided to support the protest, which was largely ignored by passers-by. Their progress was, to their surprise, halted by a large contingent of gardaí, who proceeded to attack them when Browne requested permission to hold a peaceful protest at the US Embassy. He was violently assaulted and hurled to the ground by a burly policeman. Then he and the other marchers were forced back to Clare Street, where they were set upon by savage Alsatian police dogs. Many of the protesters, including Browne, were bitten and some of them required hospital treatment for their injuries. This notorious attack by police and dogs on peaceful protesters was widely reported and condemned; and a photograph of a dog attacking Noël Browne was published in the national newspapers the following day.

The event resulted in a court case, in which it was alleged by the Gardaí that the marchers had actually provoked the police dogs. One positive outcome of the trial was the conclusion that savage police dogs should not be used again in peaceful situations such as this. Frank

O'Connor, the highly regarded author and veteran of the War of Independence, was so incensed by the use of the dogs against a peaceful protest that he suggested another march be held to demonstrate the right of citizens to protest peacefully. He led the demonstration, which was a silent and peaceful event that attracted tens of thousands of people of all political allegiances and none. It brought together many concerned citizens wishing to assert their fundamental right to peaceful protest.

The NPD had been established in 1958 by Noël Browne and Jack McQuillan after ten futile years of attempting to achieve serious progress on critical health and related social issues in the Dáil. Browne had entered politics not as an ideological socialist (and he was never a communist) but as a concerned doctor who passionately wanted to do something meaningful about the scourge of TB in Ireland. His political experiences had certainly radicalised him and convinced him that the implementation of meaningful reforms required far more fundamental change in the political system. He had therefore become a 'dangerous socialist'. The political parties he tried to influence may have changed, but his personal socialist convictions appeared to grow stronger with each setback. In certain respects, he was a harbinger of many changes that were to come to pass in Ireland later and which continue to influence politics up to the present day.

Browne had a difficult and troubled upbringing in a family who had first-hand experience of hardship and TB. His father, who was from a small farming background in County Galway, was at one time a member of the RIC (the Royal Irish Constabulary). He moved to Derry from Waterford to work in a shirt factory after Noël's birth in 1915. His mother was a devout Catholic who had eight children, one of whom died of tuberculous meningitis in infancy, and who herself died in her early forties. Most of his childhood was spent in Athlone, where his father, who died at the early age of 54, was an inspector dealing with the prevention of cruelty to children. Noël himself, his father, his mother and two of his sisters were victims of TB. After the death of both parents, the children, now orphans and in very poor circumstances, had to travel to England to be cared for by their eldest sister, Eileen. After the war, Browne, now a doctor, and his wife, Phyllis, returned to Ireland from Britain, with the desire to work towards some form of socialised medicine. The welfare state in Britain was in its infancy and Browne knew that the benefits of a universal health care system could be transformative in Ireland.

He was persuaded by Noel Hartnett, a lawyer and former friend of de Valera, and a Fianna Fáil member, to join Clann na Poblachta, which, under Seán MacBride, the son of Maud Gonne MacBride, appeared to be the most radical option available at the time. It had its origins in the republican movement, but was now, given the many people disillusioned with the three main parties of the state, intent on building a strong political force.

Browne launched the Mother and Child Scheme in 1948, when he was the new Minister for Health in the State's first coalition government, which was made up of Fine Gael, Labour and Clann na Poblachta. He did sterling work in tackling and virtually eradicating TB from the state by transforming the earlier, inadequate approaches to that devastating disease. However, because of his political inexperience, or perhaps his lack of political regimentation, he stumbled into many confrontations with the most powerful forces in Irish society, including the leader of his own party, Seán MacBride. He had become Minister for Health in a country where health, education and welfare were largely controlled by the Catholic Church and where, more than two decades after the creation of the State, no independent Department of Health had been established. The Mother and Child Scheme was essentially a government proposal to amend the Fianna Fáil Health Act 1947. The scheme would provide full medical care for mothers before and after childbirth, an entirely free family doctor medical consultancy service, free hospital care for all children up to 16, home visits by a midwife, etc. When Browne's proposals were first published, they were warmly welcomed by the other parties in government. They were also widely supported by the general public and one prelate, Dr Dignan, who was Bishop of Clonfert and Chairman of the National Insurance Board.

However, when the Church hierarchy, the medical profession and Archbishop John Charles McQuaid decided to oppose the scheme, it became 'Dr Noël Browne's Scheme' and he became a public scapegoat.

In his book *Against the Tide*, Noël Browne pointed out that the hierarchy's views on many of the issues in the scheme were set out in a letter of 6 September 1947 to de Valera, just before he left office, expressing their disapproval of the 1947 Fianna Fáil Health Act. Browne quoted from that important letter a passage which read:

> *For the state, under the Act, to empower the public authorities to provide for the health of all children, and to treat their ailments, and to educate women in regard to health, and to provide them with gynaecological services, was directly and entirely contrary to Catholic social teaching, the rights of the family, the rights of the Church in education and the rights of the medical profession and the voluntary institutions.*

This letter was written and sent before Dr Browne even entered government as Minister for Health, though much greater hostility was to follow during his short period in office. Totally isolated and deserted by colleagues in the coalition, he had to tender his resignation as Minister for Health in April 1951. In his book *Noël Browne*, John Horgan describes him as a 'passionate outsider', which he was: outside a political system that was deeply flawed and a hostage to a conservative political system that was in fear of the Catholic hierarchy.

Much has been written, some less than favourable, about Browne, his personality and his complex political journey. There was no easy, straightforward route in the Irish Republic at that time for a man passionate about change, a man who was not satisfied with complaining about the health system as a left-wing outsider, but who wanted to be where he could exercise the maximum power so as to make a real difference to people's lives.

Under the jurisdiction of the bishops, the religious orders ran the hospitals and nursing homes, trained the nurses, employed the doctors and surgeons, owned the properties and dictated the costs. They had similarly extensive control of schools and colleges, mother and baby homes, orphanages and teacher training centres; and they wanted minimal state supervision of their activities. Where welfare was concerned, they had a preference for Church-run charities over public service provision. They were particularly opposed to free or no-means-test services, paid for by the taxpayers, as being entirely contrary to Catholic social teaching. Browne's difficult personal and political journey from 1947 was indicative of the major challenges facing anyone seeking to achieve some modicum of equality and social justice in the Irish Republic.

Meanwhile, everyone in the Geraghty family knew only too well how destructive the curse of TB was among poor working-class families. They had seen it in the Liberties, which was one of the major locations for the disease. While their direct family had escaped its ravages, because of the vigilance and care of their parents, they had relatives who became infected and they saw other families devastated by the absence of an adequate response. They also knew that there was a widespread fear of admitting to the disease, as there was a fear that it might endanger the prospects of other family members. None of them was in any doubt about the direct links between poverty, unemployment, access to proper healthcare, diagnostic and treatment facilities, and substandard housing in the spread of the disease. These were some of the reasons why four of the Geraghty family – Tom, Sé, Des and Hugh – became active members of the NPD at that time.

In the early years of the 1960s, there was evidence of a new awakening in Ireland and across the world on many contentious issues affecting people's rights and opportunities. In the United States, 'We Shall Overcome' had become the anthem of the black civil rights movement, a call that had echoes everywhere. In the UK, the Ban the Bomb movement and various anti-racist groups were increasingly active. The twin international campaigns against the Vietnam War and apartheid in South Africa were growing in momentum. Various women's groups were actively challenging inequality and sexism in society. In Ireland, we had an emerging Housing Action Campaign, as well as the civil rights movement in the North. Sinn Féin, having recognised the futility of border campaigns against partition, had begun to focus on major social issues which, they hoped, would unite people of different persuasions in pursuit of their common aspirations.

During that period, both Noël Browne and Jack McQuillan were political catalysts and advocates for change. As party members, or as independents, they both made a major contribution to changing attitudes in Ireland on most progressive issues. From 1963 they worked as members of the Labour Party at a time when there was a resurgence of interest in working-class issues and socialist ideas.

Even Brendan Corish was proclaiming that 'the 70s would be socialist', although it later became evident that many socialists would be 70 and still waiting for socialism. Mrs Gaj's restaurant and the pubs in Baggot Street became Ireland's answer to Bob Dylan's 'music in the cafés at night and revolution in the air'. Des and many of his friends were frequent visitors to both. Gaj's restaurant became the nerve centre of constituency work for Noël Browne, now a Labour Party TD for Dublin South-East. It later became the focal point for discourse and dissension, with the Women's Liberation Movement making good use of the café and the basement printing press to produce radical campaigning literature.

Although the Labour Party was successful in attracting some major heavyweights, such as Conor Cruise O'Brien, David Thornley, Justin Keating, Catherine McGuinness, John O'Connell, Brendan Halligan, Michael D. Higgins, Frank Cluskey, Barry Desmond, Michael O'Leary, Jim Kemmy, Mary Robinson and many more, it still seemed unable to break fully with the Civil War mould of Irish politics. The only alternative to perpetual Fianna Fáil domination was seen as a coalition with Fine Gael, which was increasingly considering 'the just society' and, later, Garret FitzGerald's 'constitutional crusade'. A considerable minority, including Noël Browne, Brendan Scott and their supporters in the party, opposed the idea of coalition with Fine Gael and became 'collateral damage' in the scramble for power.

As early as 1971, Browne made political waves with a speech in Tramore, County Waterford, in which he said, 'No one can seriously doubt that the Catholic Church has behaved to all our political parties in the identical way as the Orange Order in its control of the Unionist Party in the North – a sectarian and bigoted politically conservative pressure group.' That statement won him few friends in the Labour Party and in April Brendan Corish, leader of the Labour Party, speaking on behalf of the whole parliamentary party, denounced and disowned Browne's views. Nor was Browne's popularity in that quarter enhanced when, in 1972, he suggested that Ireland was not the 'terrible beauty' of Yeats, but 'had become a sectarian, angry and repressive old crone'.

In 1979, Browne put down approximately forty amendments to Charles Haughey's controversial and sectarian Family Planning Bill and in 1980 he tabled in the Seanad a Private Members' Bill on divorce; yet no representative, male or female, supported his proposals.

The rejection of the views of Dr Noël Browne as Minister for Health and as a genuine, progressive moderniser in the Republic left Ireland with a legacy of serious political problems, many of which remain to be resolved satisfactorily. These include serious incidence of low pay and poverty, a major gap between rich and poor, many destitute communities overwhelmed by drug addiction and crime, an inadequate and underfunded health service, a discriminatory two-tier health system, and sectarian control of medical services, hospitals, schools, colleges, mother and baby homes, orphanages, teacher training colleges and many charities.

Every advance in the rights of citizens to full gender equality, contraception, divorce, abortion, adoption rights and birth information has had to be campaigned and fought for over and over again. The idea of a truly open and tolerant society still often seems a distant mirage. Yet there is growing hope that a more open and diverse country could be capable of achieving the truly egalitarian and caring 'republic of equals' for which so many have hoped for and worked for so tirelessly.

11

Good for Geraghty

When the Union's inspiration through the workers' blood
shall run,
There can be no power greater anywhere beneath the sun.
Yet what force on earth is weaker than the feeble strength
of one?
But the Union makes us strong.
          - *Solidarity Forever by Ralph Chaplin, 1915*

Seán was the eldest of the family and from an early age he was recognised as someone not to be trifled with. He was tough, courageous and dependable in a way that was not often spoken of, but you always knew to be true. While three of the boys – Tom, Sé and Des – won Dublin Corporation Scholarships to secondary school, at first in James Street CBS, Seán took up an apprenticeship in Hammond Lane Foundries. He loved the mountains and hiking, and he spent a lot of his spare time cycling, camping or hostelling with his many friends and with his brothers, particularly Tom, in An Óige, the youth hostelling association.

When the family moved to Drimnagh, Seán became an active member of Na Fianna Éireann and rose to be the officer in command (OC) of the Franshaw House sluagh (branch) at the top of the Crumlin Road. He met many good friends there who were to remain close friends for the rest of his life. Not particularly noted for sailing or seamanship by other members of the family, Seán surprised them by joining the Naval Reserve. He attended training camps involving maritime activities and military training in Haulbowline in County Cork.

Later he became involved in the 1956 IRA border campaign. No one else in the family had been aware of his intentions, but they later learned that he was part of the Joe Crystle and Liam Kelly Saor Uladh, a breakaway group from the IRA, which was among the earliest groups to begin armed raids across the border in that ill-advised 1950s campaign. He was eventually arrested by the Gardaí, charged in Dublin and sentenced to a term in Mountjoy. In jail, Seán somehow managed to 'acquire' a serious appendix problem and was transferred to the Mater Hospital for urgent treatment. With the help of an apparently affectionate young woman who clung closely to him on their way out, while a group of visitors stood around his bed in the ward, he made a daring and amorous escape past an unsuspecting Special Branch officer guarding the door of the ward.

Seán quickly disappeared from view after that escape and remained under cover until the Northern border campaign was well and truly over. That experience certainly appeared to convince him that future armed forays across the Irish border would never succeed in ending partition in Ireland. He became keenly aware that a large part of the Northern Ireland population wished to remain British and that situation could not be resolved easily by a physical force campaign rooted in the Republic. Through his union activities in the British labour movement, Seán developed many staunch English, Scottish and Welsh supporters and friends. However, he never relented on his personal conviction that the division of his own country was an unacceptable assault by the British on the people of Ireland through their 'divide and conquer' policy in 1921.

It appears that Seán spent some more time on the run in Ireland after his escape from custody, later making his way to Scotland. About a year later, the family was visited by a tall, dignified and kilted Scottish nationalist, from a large property-owning clan, who assured Mrs Geraghty and family that Seán was safe and well and living happily somewhere in the highlands of Scotland.

Later, Seán made his way to London and linked up with some of his cousins, including Pat O'Neill, an industrial officer in the Electrical Trades Union. He soon made many other Irish friends, such as Seán Furlong, the eldest brother of the Furlong/Behan family, who was active in the labour movement in London at the time. Dominic Behan was also a friend in the UK – he was making a career as a singer, songwriter and folk music collector, as was the uilleann piper Séamus Ennis, one of our finest traditional musicians, who got some work as a collector for the BBC. When visiting London, Seán also met for many an enjoyable pint with Luke Kelly, a fellow friend and Dubliner.

In London, Seán and his brother Tom, who joined him there, were part of a formidable array of former republicans and Irish socialists who had taken temporary refuge in Britain. Curiously enough, they found themselves living reasonably well at the heart of the ancient oppressor, since employment was scarce in Ireland and their life choices had been strictly limited in their own deficient Republic. Irish people were so numerous in London in the fifties and sixties that their regularly articulated demand for the return of the six counties was often met with the good-natured response from their English comrades, 'Yes, certainly … and give us back Camden Town'!

It is perhaps interesting to note that over the centuries, Irish emigrants have made a major and disproportionate contribution to the development of the trade union movement in Britain, the USA and Australia. When arriving as migrants, they often found allies among other disadvantaged groups, particularly in their places of work. Many found they had a natural ability to organise, campaign and lead their fellow workers in struggles for better conditions. The East London and Liverpool dockers, the Pittsburg miners, the New York transport workers, Boston labourers, Chicago meat workers and Australian seamen all produced strong Irish leaders in their trade unions.

It was clear to Des that in Britain, many workers of different nationality, colour or gender would readily support their work colleagues when strong leadership and clear anti-sectarian direction was evident. The demand for one rate for the job, irrespective of where you came from, was the key for the trade unions to build that solidarity. It was equally evident that migrant rates, or migrant segregation in employment by unscrupulous employers, can cultivate serious anti-migrant racism.

Over years of working in the electrical sector and in Fleet Street with the various newspaper electricians, Seán Geraghty developed a very strong reputation as an elected union representative and an effective negotiator. He helped to enhance wages and working conditions in the electrical and newsprint sectors and as a consequence had no difficulty securing election year after year as secretary of his union branch.

The relatively well-paid workers in Seán's branch frequently supported other workers in solidarity disputes, notably Arthur Scargill and the National Union of Mineworkers (NUM) in their dispute with Mrs Thatcher and the National Coal Board following pit closures in 1984–85. That strike was generally considered the most bitter industrial dispute in British history. The Fleet Street electricians and many other workers, including those in Ireland, America and elsewhere, supported the miners with generous financial help. Seán had many difficulties in his own union because of his unflinching support for the miners' cause. While he was a firm supporter of the NUM, Seán was always uneasy about Scargill's leadership, because of his brash temperament and poor strategic thinking. Scargill did not appear to consult enough with more experienced colleagues in the various regions of the NUM. There was also a constant worry about the absence of a complete and verifiable national strike ballot. This issue later proved to be part of Scargill's Achilles heel, when the dispute was dealt with in the law courts. It also negatively affected the views of other categories of workers in sectors and grades close to the mining industry. That evident weakness resulted in related unions and workers in the coal industry not supporting the dispute.

It was evident that Prime Minister Margaret Thatcher and the National Coal Board had anticipated this confrontation and had built up coal stocks long before the dispute even began. Thatcher had clearly resolved to smash the NUM because it was the most powerful trade union in the UK at the time and had successfully faced down the Conservative government in 1972 and 1974, which had led to the fall of the Conservative government led by Ted Heath.

During the 1970s disputes, the NUM had won the widespread support of the steel workers, rail workers and port workers. Arthur Scargill had established his reputation through the use of 'flying pickets', who targeted particularly sensitive locations where the strikers needed support. In 1983, the law on secondary picketing had changed, dramatically weakening the power of the unions. Thatcher appointed Ian MacGregor as Chief Executive of the National Coal Board. He was a hard-line Thatcherite who had successfully scaled down the nationalised British Steel Industry and facilitated the privatisation of the remainder. He helped her defeat the NUM in the 1984–85 dispute with his uncompromising approach and, as a consequence, seriously weakened the power of the NUM, the strongest and most militant union in Britain.

Two years earlier, the nurses and ancillary workers in the National Health Service had served a pay claim for a 12% increase, because of serious low pay and poor working conditions in the service. Jim Prior MP, a member of Mrs Thatcher's government in 1979 and Secretary of State for Employment, disagreed with some of her extreme anti-trade union and monetary policies. In 1980 he introduced an Industrial Relations Act, which the Prime Minister believed was not tough enough, but which subsequently became an important factor in the nurses' dispute. In 1981, Prior was removed by Thatcher from his position as Secretary for Employment and replaced by Norman Tebbit, a loyal Thatcherite. Prior was demoted and moved to the role of Secretary for Northern Ireland, despite his reluctance to leave his critically important cabinet post.

There was considerable sympathy for the nurses among both the trade unions and the general public. The TUC passed resolutions of support for the nurses and urged support for their cause. Rodney Bickerstaffe, general secretary of the National Union of Public Employees (NUPE), pointed out that 'It is working people who are cared for by the National Health Service and it is they we are protecting. We demand that the rest of the trade union movement, all of it, rallies around and supports our fight.' Some unions and groups of workers responded with decisions to take supportive action, but the employers secured injunctions under the 1980 Act to prevent these secondary

actions. The big concern of many union executives was the poten-
tially punitive fines that could be imposed on them if the strikes went
ahead. Seán Geraghty and the Fleet Street electricians branch decided
to support the nurses in their dispute by holding a one-day strike,
which would stop the production of all the national papers. They
ignored the injunction of the Newspaper Publishers' Association and
proceeded with their stoppage, which was 100% effective.

As a consequence, the employers immediately instigated a court
action against Seán Geraghty for his failure to comply with the injunction. For the next few days, the police had to conduct a 'hide and seek'
game with him as they could not locate him in order to serve their
writ, or give him the notice of court proceeding. This involved visits
to his home and a tour of likely public houses in the vicinity of Fleet
Street. Eventually, after a few days, the fugitive was found having a
quiet pint in a local pub; he asked them, 'What took you so long?' Seán
was arrested and taken into custody.

In the High Court, Seán told Mr Justice Leonard that his union
branch was a democratic one whose members had voted for strike
action, so only they could reverse that decision. The judge said he had
underestimated his powers and could have tried to stop the strike
after he was ordered to do so by an injunction taken out by the newspaper proprietors. He also said it was a tragedy that the law had come
into collision with Mr Geraghty, but added that the tragedy lay at Mr
Geraghty's door. The judge fined him £350 and awarded legal costs
(about £5,000) against him. He gave him two months to pay or he
would have to spend a week in prison. The employers considered that
they had a claim for losses of around £2–4 million in damages, but
were reluctant to pursue a claim they knew would be totally unre-
alistic. Already they were on public notice that if Seán Geraghty was
jailed, there would be more and wider work stoppages by many trade
union members in all parts of the country.

The nurses had taken to the streets across the country, carrying
banners declaring: 'GOOD FOR GERAGHTY – WOULD YOU JAIL
SOMEONE FOR SUPPORTING NURSES?' Thousands gathered in
support of the nurses at a TUC-organised rally outside the Department of Health at the Elephant and Castle in London, at which

Seán Geraghty was an invited speaker, as was Rodney Bickerstaffe. Seán was greeted with tumultuous applause from the thousands of demonstrators.

Lord Marsh, Chairman of the Newspaper Publishers' Association, who had brought the action against Geraghty, recognised the cautious decision of the judge as a 'sophisticated, highly intelligent reaction to this particular problem. We all know the difficulty of dealing with industrial relations through the courts.' He was well aware that a decision to jail Seán would have had major repercussions, including widespread work stoppages, which the employers did not want.

While Seán was successful on this occasion, he had much more difficult and far less rewarding outcomes in later years when the media magnate Rupert Murdoch closed his publications in Fleet Street and moved operations to an ultra-modern facility in Wapping. With the use of new technology and active collaboration by some union leaders in the Electrical Trades Union, the power of the Fleet Street electricians was completely undermined.

The labour movement generally considered Seán Geraghty's stand during the nurses' strike and the court judgment as a setback to the anti-union agenda of Tebbit and Thatcher. As a result, an independent health service pay review was conducted, which produced significant improvements for nurses and healthcare workers. Unfortunately, this outcome did not halt Thatcher's determined onslaught against the trade unions. The outcome of her conflict with the miners, two years later, was to produce a far less satisfactory outcome for the trade union movement.

Rodney Bickerstaffe and his colleagues became Seán's close friends and allies during many years of industrial relations activity in Britain. In 1993, Rodney became general secretary of UNISON, the largest amalgamated trade union in Britain, with 1.3 million members. He was highly regarded as a campaigner for the lower-paid and for the introduction of a national minimum wage, a concept not supported by most UK unions at that time. The *Guardian* newspaper described him as 'a highly thoughtful, pragmatic and strategic leader'. He supported the NUM during their difficulties and worked tirelessly, but unfortunately in vain, with Bill Keys of the Society of Graphical and Allied Trades (SOGAT) towards resolving the 1984–85 miners' strike.

In a strange quirk of fate, Rodney's mother, Elizabeth, a former nurse, who reared him alone until she married when he was 11 years old, told him shortly before her death in the 1990s that his father was a Tommy Simpson from Dublin and that his birth in 1945 had arisen from a brief war-time romance. His father had returned home to Ireland shortly after the war and had lost contact with her over the years. Later, on a visit to Dublin for a union conference which ended early, Rodney used the few details his mother had given him to check out a particular address. He did not meet anyone at that address, but a neighbour directed him to another house on a nearby street. There the door was opened by a look-alike half-brother. There were two other half-brothers, all of whom gave him a warm welcome. A curious aspect of this discovery was that one of Rodney's newly discovered half-brothers in the Simpson family had a long-standing trade union involvement and was well known to the Geraghty family in Dublin. As a consequence, Des, his partner, Rosheen, and his brother Tom had the great pleasure of attending the first family reunion as dinner guests, along with Rodney and all his long-lost Dublin relatives. Even Tony Blair, the British Prime Minister, was publicly congratulated Rodney on the happy discovery of his long-lost family in Dublin.

12

Winds of Change

The winds of change began to blow strongly in Ireland in the 1960s. Initially they were small, intermittent squalls, well dispersed and easily weathered by our deeply conservative establishment. Yet, as the decade progressed, those squalls became stronger and more unrelenting, at times even reaching gale force and beginning to shake the very foundations of the State. It was as though a force of nature had begun to unleash the pent-up energy of the people that had been suppressed for far too long and it was now furiously escaping and creating an exciting, if turbulent, atmosphere in the country. It was increasingly infecting the whole body politic, permeating the economic and social life of a country that had languished in the doldrums for far too long.

Ireland was not alone. British politicians had begun to talk about the winds of change blowing across Africa; and this was certainly the case from Cyprus to South Africa and even within the previously monolithic and expansionist Soviet Union. They were beginning to create serious storms in individual states such as Hungary and Poland, but also in the Balkans. South East Asia was also erupting, breaking out of its colonial past and challenging the old imperial controls of the European states of Britain, France, Spain, Portugal and Italy. There was also growing resistance to the more recently established global hegemony of the United States. In many countries, where there were oppressors and oppressed, people were now challenging the old order and seeking a new and more equal kind of world – one that was not yet clearly defined and certainly not yet fully understood.

For Ireland, the decade began with the problems of economic stagnation, high unemployment and massive emigration, major inequality, cultural isolationism, anti-intellectualism and lots of sexual taboos and repression of women. Change was certainly in the air.

The Secretary of the Department of Finance, T.K. Whitaker, an economist and a lover of the Irish language, challenged Seán Lemass, the new leader of Fianna Fáil, and President Éamon de Valera, to implement a new economic policy of free trade and increased emphasis on foreign investment. This later became known the First Programme for Economic Expansion. The Lemass government of 1959–66 accepted Whitaker's advice on a programme which had a 2% growth target, although it actually achieved 4%. That government also established an Irish television station, relaxed somewhat the censorship of books and films and invested much more in education. The political decisions of that decade of the 1960s are rightly considered historic milestones on the journey towards the development of the modern Irish state.

At a more basic level, an increasingly egalitarian atmosphere was beginning to emerge in Irish society, in particular in the pubs and entertainment centres, in the universities and theatres, at musical events, in broadcasting, in radio and television. Young people were travelling more, leaving the cities to enjoy the freedom and personal liberation associated with the Fleadh Cheoil or major outdoor musical events. As many former emigrants returned to avail of new jobs, they brought back a flavour of their lives in more open societies. Irish television was making waves in the old stagnant pools of Irish conservatism. In Dublin, a few avant-garde pubs and restaurants in the south inner city became places for more open conversation about politics and other social concerns. A rejuvenated intellectual life became a more normal feature of these establishments, which was a welcome departure from the dreary 1950s. This process continued across the country, north, south, east and west, spurred on by the arrival of the new Irish television service, which was providing more information, greater diversity of opinions and new and interesting insights into both local issues and the wider world.

One of the most interesting pubs in Dublin was McDaid's of Harry Street, off Grafton Street, which Sé Geraghty, his brother Des and their cousins Mattie and Christy O'Neill often frequented on weekend nights. An alternative local bar for any overspill was Neary's in Chatham Street, where opera singers or concert performers from the Gaiety Theatre, or late-night performers at the Grafton Cinema folk sessions could rub shoulders with the great unwashed of the city. Among the many regulars in McDaid's were well-known poets, students, actors, artists, writers, broadcasters and the odd member of the landed gentry or business class. Paddy Kavanagh and Catherine Barry were frequent visitors, as were the Behan and Furlong clan when they were in town. This was a very democratic drinking institution where Paddy O'Brien, the manager, kept the best of order and, when required, mediated in volatile situations likely to disrupt the convivial atmosphere of the institution.

No class of person was exonerated from the unwritten rules for 'good order and respect for the management'. On one occasion, Brendan Behan tested that good order and was asked to leave when he launched a diatribe of abuse against Paddy Kavanagh, the 'bog-man' at the bar. This was just one minor episode in a widely reported public spat between the two eminent writers which kept the general populace entertained for a number of years. Eventually, Brendan, in deference to his good friend Paddy O'Brien, withdrew reluctantly from the fray and made his way with some friends to the Bailey pub in Duke Street, which was managed by another long-suffering and tolerant host, John Ryan.

Within a short period of time there was a whole network of drinking venues where people would congregate to share common interests. 'The Strip' – Merrion Row and Lower Baggot Street – became Dublin's emerging Left Bank. O'Donoghue's became the home of the balladeers, Ronnie Drew and the Dubliners, Ted Furey, the McKennas and many musicians, plus a mix of stray Americans. O'Neill's across the road took O'Donoghue's spillover. This was an old-style and well-ordered establishment, which attracted politicos, Gaeilgeoirí, journalists and broadcasters. Doheny and Nesbitt's became the venue for politicians and economists; and Toner's a refuge for those displaced from other overcrowded establishments. It has been said that there can be no revolution without its poets, its songs and its revolutionaries. The sixties seemed to have all these elements cavorting together in one small part of Dublin city.

Mrs Gaj's restaurant in Baggot Street was the place for reasonable food at affordable prices; it became the central meeting place for female campaigners, left-wing or republican activists and supporters of Dr Noël Browne, be they Labour Party members or unattached admirers. In the later sixties, a good number of American draft dodgers and peace campaigners also flooded into the area. Another impressive arrival was Deirdre O'Connell, a beautiful American singer and theatre director who established her new, radical Stanislavski Focus Theatre in Pembroke Street, which was regularly supported by Luke Kelly and the other Dubliners. Early participants in that venture included Sabina Coyne, later the wife of Michael D. Higgins, Tom Hickey, Áine Ní Mhuirí, Johnny Murphy, Meryl Gourley and many other fine, talented actors who greatly enhanced the reputation of the theatre in Ireland.

During the sixties there were a number of pubs in the general Grafton Street–Baggot Street area where the movers and shakers of the city, the poets, painters and revolutionaries, were likely to congregate. These establishments could be overwhelmed by certain highly opinionated characters all demanding attention for their current campaign issues and urgent priorities.

On one occasion Donal Foley, deputy editor of the *Irish Times* and author of the Myles na gCopaleen-type 'Man Bites Dog' columns, who enjoyed a quiet pint after work, proposed that his friends subscribe to a small fund. This would be to employ an agile public house runner, who might keep him informed about who was drinking where, so he might know the premises to avoid.

It was evident that a new element of a more open and inclusive Ireland had arrived, even on the well-worn bar stools of the old city pubs. Some of these institutions were, surprisingly, beginning to allow live music and song. They were even allowing women to leave their snugs and join the men in the previously taboo corners of the premises. The Irish genie was certainly out of the bottle and it was quite evident that it would be impossible for anyone to ever try putting it back in again.

The sixties was the decade of campaigns and the members of the Geraghty family were, unsurprisingly, participants in most of them. A remarkable number of national and international causes inspired the concerned younger generations to become involved. There were never enough days to meet the needs of these demanding activities.

The early concern about the nuclear threat was followed by war and peace campaigns. The black civil rights campaigns in the USA stirred the conscience of many and brought a greater focus on racism and human rights. Irish republicans in the South began vigorous campaigns against ground rents, a hangover from the colonial landlord era, as well as for fishing rights on rural rivers, small farmers' rights and for action on the never-ending housing problems, particularly in the cities.

When the Americans replaced the French in Vietnam, Ireland had a very active movement called the Irish Voice on Vietnam. Des served on the committee of Ireland's Voice on Vietnam for the whole duration of that awful war. The Irish Anti-Apartheid Movement, under Louise and Kader Asmal, gained huge support across all political parties, as did the Northern Irish Civil Rights Movement. Other campaigns also developed, such as Coiste Cearta Sibialta na Gaeltachta (Gaeltacht Civil Rights) and the Travellers' Rights campaigns. In the latter part of the decade, a strong and influential Women's Liberation Movement emerged which set in motion major changes in Irish life. That women's movement became the forerunner of other campaigns, including, in more recent times, the LGBT+ movement, which also grew considerably in the following decades. It was as though the whole country was marching to the strains of Bob Dylan's evocative song in which he said that the answer to so many questions was 'Blowin' in the Wind':

How many years must a mountain exist,
Before it is washed to the sea?
And how many years can a people exist,
Before they're allowed to be free?
The answer, my friend, is blowin' in the wind
The answer is blowin' in the wind.

Young Tom in his youth was the most rambunctious member of the family, a lover of sport and an inspirational singer. He loved football and all kinds of sports and physical activity, well marked by daily evidence of bloody wounds and bruises. He helped Des to learn to swim in the Grand Canal, initially in the dark waters of the canal basin at the James Street Harbour, or, as described in the old song 'The Wreck of the Bogaboo', the 'James Street Ship Canal'. This historic watercourse, once a major commercial route from the Shannon and the Midland bogs to the city, was not just the only place to swim. It was also a great source of comic verse about the trials and tribulations of dryland bargemen 'braving the stormy seas' on their heavily laden vessels. And it was heavily polluted with oil and diesel discharges from the barges and industry in the area. Now, all the musically celebrated hazards have disappeared under a hard blanket of city concrete, all the way to Rialto Bridge, which facilitated the building of the Luas. There, it used to join the main water route of the Grand Canal between east and west. Now, alas, the risks are only for landlubbers, commuting much more speedily from Saint James's Hospital along the Back of the Pipes to such exotic places as Rialto, Drimnagh, Clondalkin or the sprawling suburbs of Tallaght.

In those days the young city swimmers had very little awareness of water pollution in the canal basin. But in retrospect, the clearer waters were always in competition with dark pools of oil slick, discharged regularly by the canal barges that used to frequent those 'stormy waters'. Later swimmers gravitated to clearer waters, to the iron bridge or to Goldenbridge; or at a push they might undertake the long bicycle ride out to Williamstown, near Blackrock. The overcrowded indoor swimming pools in Tara Street, or in the Iveagh Buildings, became the only swimming options during the wet and windy weather of autumn and winter.

When the tide was out at Williamstown, it often seemed so far out that it would feel almost like walking to Wales in order to paddle your feet. The next nearest option was Seapoint, a short bit further south. That regular exertion not only made swimmers of the boys, but also hardy cyclists. This stood to them as they later took to travelling the whole country, camping and hiking in such far-flung places as Donegal, Kerry, Wicklow, Galway, Mayo and Sligo.

When Tom emigrated to London in 1957, after achieving a good Leaving Cert in James's Street CBS, he was greatly missed by the younger members of the family, Sé, Des and Hugh. For a considerable time before going, he had sought suitable employment in Dublin, particularly in the printing industry, but without success. Emigration was the only option for him and thousands more.

Since Tom's grandfather had been a member of the Typographical Society and had worked for a number of well-established companies, his father, Tom, thought that the print trade might be a good option for him. He was disappointed to discover that grandfathers didn't count any more. Only the sons of printers could be considered for apprenticeships, according to the union rules in those days. After various rejections in relation to any worthwhile job opportunities in Dublin, the disappointed Tom headed off with a heavy heart to London to look for employment and to join his friend and older brother, Seán.

In Cornmarket, Tom and the neighbouring boys loved to play football. Even when no playing field was available in the Liberties, they would play in Lamb Alley, with a large rubber ball. Soccer was the game of the streets and Gaelic or hurling were the games the Christian Brothers organised in school. The nearest Gaelic playing fields were in Dolphin's Barn, a few miles away, but a street game of soccer could be played in Lamb Alley, a quiet side street beside the Iveagh Market, with little passing traffic. That didn't deter the local gardaí from unrelentingly chasing the players, confiscating their rubber ball, or at worst actually booking the children and summoning them to answer charges in the Children's Court.

On one occasion, a sizeable group of local children was rounded up and summonsed for the crime of playing street football. When their day in court arrived, Lily Geraghty, Tom's mother, attended the court with the other mothers and challenged the Gardaí and the judge for 'making criminals out of young children' who were deprived of the opportunity to play ball because there were no proper facilities. After Lily's impassioned address to the surprised judge, he dismissed all cases and wondered why the authorities were not providing any proper sports facilities for inner-city children. Mrs Geraghty's standing among the neighbours of Cornmarket, High Street and Francis Street was sky-high after that historic football score: 1–0 to the working class. One of the 'football criminals' was a young Reed from Liverpool, a grandson of Whack Reid, a docker relative of the family who had served in Boland's Mill under de Valera in 1916. Another member of that family, Peter Reid, subsequently became a famous soccer star, manager of Manchester City, among other teams, and a well-known TV soccer pundit in Britain.

In London, Tom came to live in Highbury, next to the famous Gunners in the Arsenal Stadium. There he was able to indulge his interest in soccer and later, as chairman of the South O'Hanlon's Gaelic Athletic Association (GAA) club in London, to promote Gaelic games. It's perhaps worth remembering that the sporting youth of Dublin city paid little heed to the restrictive GAA ban on 'foreign' games and played whatever they could, when and where they could, without reference to such admonitions from on high. That tradition of openness to many sports was also alive and well among our emigrant population.

Those were not the only games Tom played as he launched himself into trade union and left-wing politics in London. The city was alive with radical politics and a myriad of competing groups following a variety of routes to their hoped-for promised land. The Irish were well represented in this milieu with papers and pamphlets, as were all the tendencies of the left. There were active socialists, anarchists, communists, people of different religious persuasions and all the races, creeds and colours seeking support for their individual causes. There were also many active Irish organisations in Britain at that time, with their own supporters, papers and publications. Tom and his friends were part of a small group called the Irish Workers' Group, with their own newspaper, the *Irish Worker*, which Tom edited for some time. It attracted some diverse contributors, people like John Palmer, Liam Dalton, Phil Flynn, Pat O'Donovan, Dick Walsh and others.

When he came back to Dublin from London in 1963 to take up employment in the Dublin Fire Brigade, Tom was soon busily engaged in trade union activity as a member of the Federated Workers' Union of Ireland (FWUI), or Larkin's union, which represented most of the Fire Brigade personnel. He became a local representative, a branch committee member and eventually a member of the National Executive Council of the union. Some of Tom's early achievements were the establishment of pay parity between the Fire Brigade personnel and the Gardaí, reduced working hours, and extra payment for working bank holidays, or time off or payments in lieu. There was a happy family convergence in 1990 when the ITGWU and the FWUI merged to form SIPTU – the Services, Industrial, Professional and Technical Union – with Tom on the new National Executive Council and his brother Des a national industrial officer and later general president of the united union.

Tom, with Trevor Whitehead, carried out a number of years of painstaking research and compilation to produce a comprehensive historical record of the Dublin Fire Brigade from its earliest days to modern times, published by the Dublin City Council. He gave particular attention to establishing strong relationships with other fire service personnel in Ireland and but also those in such distant locations as Belfast, Scotland and the USA. When many New York colleagues and friends were killed in the 9/11 attack, Tom attended formal ceremonies there on behalf of the Dublin Fire Brigade. The Irish are very well represented in the fire services of the United States and Tom was active over the years in developing a very close association between the members of the brigades in New York and Dublin.

13

Not by Bread Alone

A year before the 1913 Lock-Out in Dublin, a remarkable strike took place in the town of Lawrence in Massachusetts. The strike involved 20,000 textile workers, mostly women from at least thirty different nationalities, and also many children below the legal minimum working age of 14 years. They were being paid poverty-level wages for a 56-hour working week and endured atrocious working conditions. That tumultuous two-month strike spawned the famous slogan of the women strikers, 'Bread and Roses' – a concept that became a universal theme for women workers everywhere. For all trade unionists, it also became one of the cornerstones of their demand for a complete social wage, not only for pay but for dignity, for safety, for improved working conditions, for all the beautiful things that can enrich people's lives.

When Des was told in late 1969 that his application for employment in the ITGWU had been successful and that he was to present himself at Liberty Hall to take up an industrial role in Head Office, he was elated. This was his ideal job and Liberty Hall was where he most wanted to be. He was well aware of issues he would have to address in making a transition from idealistic campaigner to trade union official – not the most popular job in the country. Ireland was teeming with problems of inequality, low pay, unemployment and emigration, housing problems and serious class divisions. He knew that the modern trade union representatives were expected to deliver results in the here and now, not at some future time in the ideal world of their imagination.

The ITGWU was not perceived by many as the most radical union; neither was it a close match with many of Des's own socialist expectations, particularly his Larkinite views, which he knew could be a sore subject in Liberty Hall. The Larkin–O'Brien split back in 1923 had been part of a very divisive period in the history of that union. Des recognised that the history was very complex and often as much personality-driven as ideological. But he felt that the passage of time should have healed most of the wounds inflicted on the organisation and on the FWUI, of which his father had been a member and where his brother Tom was currently a prominent representative.

He was also very conscious of the view expressed in Austin Clarke's poem 'New Liberty Hall', with the devastating final line: 'Go, da, and shiver in your tenement'. This was a sentiment he understood very well, but it was not one he shared in relation to Liberty Hall. He believed that the new building could and should be a major centre of support for those in the tenements, as well a visible symbol of hope for the struggling working class of Ireland and all in the wider world of labour. Des felt that 'Bread and Roses' was an inspirational concept for the future. O'Casey had seen this spirit in Jim Larkin – 'a man of poetry, dancing and principles … a man who would put a flower in a vase on a table as well as a loaf of bread on a plate.' He also hoped that Larkin's slogan 'An Injury to One is the Concern of All' would never be forgotten in the new Liberty Hall.

Since there was no expectation of a socialist revolution any time in the near future, Des thought long and hard about a theme in James Connolly's *Axe to the Root* – the role of industrial democracy, which Connolly described as 'constructive socialism'. Connolly was hostile to exploitative capitalism and to the hostile state apparatus, but he recognised that that was only one part of the equation. As a trade union leader he worked hard to improve the immediate lot of workers in society as it was. He recognised that part of that work should be one of steadily building solid economic foundations through workplace democracy, within the ruins of an old, rotten and decaying system.

As time progressed, Des believed that such constructive work was an imperative for the trade union movement, given the changing circumstances in every employment and in every working-class community. This required greater attention to education and worker representation wherever decisions were being made about their lives. While political democracy gave citizens a vote, most of their working lives were spent in institutions where they had no democratic influence. This was a view he shared with an older colleague, John Swift of the bakers' trade union, and some other colleagues in the ICTU.

Years later, Des was delighted to read about the work and radical ideas of Mike Cooley, an Irish engineer from Tuam and a member of TASS, the clerical section of the Amalgamated Engineering Union in Britain, the same union as his brother Hugh's. He particularly loved Cooley's focus on 'liberating the human imagination' and his campaign in Lucas Aerospace for a transition 'from arms to socially useful production'. Over the years, he had learned to value such innovative initiatives more than simple pay militancy or radical rhetoric. He viewed these developments as important initiatives for expanding the vision of workers and for the unions to play an important and transformative role in the economy and society.

Standing in the hall of Liberty Hall, waiting for space on the lift to the fourteenth floor, he was approached one day by an older staff member. He later learned that this was Walter McFarlane, Branch Secretary of the Number 1 branch of the union. Walter didn't rush to take the lift but asked him if he was one of the people involved in the Housing Action Committee and other recent activities concerning civil rights in the city. Having established that he was, he asked where he was going and what was his business in Liberty Hall. Walter then told Des that Head Office wouldn't suit him and that he would be far better off in an active branch.

After a few days of induction and meetings with Head Office personnel, Michael Mullen, the union's general secretary, told Des that the Number 1 branch was actively lobbying for an extra branch assistant. He said that there were a lot of difficult industrial relations issues to be addressed in the docks, the oil and gas industries, some haulage and furniture delivery companies and some warehousing and coal yards. He also said that the branch secretary was in poor health. As a consequence, Des found himself allocated to the Number 1 branch, 'on a temporary basis'.

Des found the work of that branch productive and satisfying, and his colleagues were supportive and helpful. There were many minor disputes, such as those requiring adjudication on particular ship cargoes, to see if they qualified for 'dirty money' or 'exceptional dirty money'. There were bonuses in the coal yards, such as those for unduly heavy coal deliveries. The oil section was largely concerned with productivity issues; and the cross-channel dockers were dealing with complex decasualisation issues arising from the implementation of the Murphy Report. That report recommended an end to casual dock working and its replacement by a permanent allocation of dockers to individual companies as full-time employees. In the B&I shipping company, a major pension negotiation was under way, with considerable research required on past service, or broken and casual periods of employment. Disciplinary cases arose frequently and on occasion they could lead to dismissals or even unofficial disputes. Most of the work was located in the Dublin Port area and most days required a walk down the North Wall quay, where invariably members or shop stewards would appear for advice or consultation about their concerns. A close bond with the local representatives was extremely important and allowing a trusting relationship to develop could prove vital to resolving major disputes.

There were some funny moments, such as the day the British Rail dockers stopped work because their relatives had been stopped in the French port of Calais. They had been told in Calais that their travel passes were inappropriate and invalid at that point. Amid much heated argument between the senior management and the dockers' representatives about betrayal of the Murphy Report and so on, Des sought to make some sense of the angry and confusing arguments. He eventually established that at a major meeting in Liberty Hall to agree on decasualisation of the dock work – a move from casual to permanent assignment, or 'attachment' to particular companies – a question had been raised about free travel concessions to the continent, for staff of British Rail. Apparently, the management had assured the dockers that they would be treated equally with the clerical and administrative staff once they were 'attached' to the company. This was interpreted by the dockers as a licence to collect travel passes from all the dockers and pass them on to wives and relations for a religious visit to Lourdes. In an effort to explain the problem, the general manager pointed out that British Rail had no jurisdiction beyond Calais Port. Also, continental travel and the passes were only valid for particular, identifiable employees on British Rail services, and not for their relations. The docks shop steward replied belligerently: 'We were promised continental travel and isn't Lourdes on the continent? Where else would ye be going on the bloody continent?' With company co-operation, 'an Irish solution to an Irish problem' was eventually secured. This involved the release of the 'Irish pilgrims', with a private coach to take them to and from Lourdes and a small weekly contribution taken from the now permanently 'attached' employees of British Rail to contribute to the cost.

Another unexpected industrial relations issue erupted when a distraught female company manager rang Liberty Hall to ask what was the union agreement on 'drinking money'. Some months earlier, this woman had courageously taken responsibility for a specialist haulage company after her father-in-law, the owner, had died. Rather than closing the well-established business, she had undertaken to manage the company, with the support of its long-serving staff. Everything seemed to operate well until the Gardaí contacted her about one of their lorries being parked for hours outside a public house in a rural area. The driver and helper had been drinking inside the establishment for many hours. When she sought to impose some discipline on the individuals concerned, she was informed that this was part of a 'drinking money agreement' with the union. After a blunt telephone conversation between Des and the shop steward, it emerged that there was an occasional and informal productivity arrangement with the previous owner, to speed up loading and delivery of specialised cargo. He would allow the drivers some extra overtime payments for completing the work on time and to a high standard. This overtime payment had been translated informally into a so-called 'union agreement for drinking money', which the inexperienced manager was now expected to pay. While the bonus payment was paid, the public house time was not covered and the woman's haulage licence was then in serious jeopardy. The company was subsequently sold – with no compensation paid for the lost 'drinking money'.

In his time in the union's Number 1 branch, Des realised that this particular branch was far more than a negotiating unit for the workers. It was also a place for advice, help with difficult form-filling, support for family members in difficulty with the law and, on one occasion, for assistance with the day release of a prisoner from Mountjoy Prison. In this case, Des had to assure the prison' governor that his member had a safe and secure job to go to during his temporary day release. Another activity, which sometimes required the help of a solicitor, was representing the children of members – children who could have been involved in minor criminal activity such as stealing a car. On one occasion, the branch had to mind a member's weekly wages in the union safe because his aggressive and bullying in-laws regularly stole his pay.

Most of that branch's activity related to traditional male employ-ment in tough manual or semi-skilled sectors. One regular visitor to the branch was a very small, generally cheerful old lady, who came to collect a small monthly stipend from the union. When Des discovered that this was the heroic Rosie Hackett of 1916 fame, a retired member of the branch, he made sure to let her know how much she was valued by the union for her great work for women workers and for her impor-tant role in the struggle for national independence.

Early in his employment, Des became aware that female staff members were expected to retire when they got married, a practice also widespread in the public service. This 'marriage bar' was also catered for in the union's rule book, with a small marriage benefit for the members concerned. An issue arose when the Staff Representa-tive Council of the union took up the case of one female employee who was reluctant to retire when she married. A proposal emerged to allow for some extra time concession for the aggrieved staff member. This proposal had to be voted on by all staff. When Des received his ballot paper he decided that he could not in conscience vote for either proposal – neither the status quo nor the proposed concession – as he was absolutely opposed to any marriage bar in a trade union. He wrote his objection on the ballot paper and refused to vote for either option. When he retired, many, many years later, he was told that his protest ballot paper had been retained; and although it was a secret ballot, there was no doubt about whose ballot it was.

One of the most radical innovations in the trade union movement was the ITGWU's creation in 1971 of the Development Services Division, the DSD. This division was headed up by Paddy Clancy, an Executive Council member, employed by the Irish Productivity Centre and seconded by the union for this project. The DSD was pioneered by Michael Mullen, the general secretary at that time and a former Labour TD for Dublin. He recognised the increasing importance of education and training, research, communications (including printing and publications) and industrial engineering for union members in the changing world of work. Mullen employed high-quality professionals to head up the four disciplines and departments; and they, along with Paddy Clancy, assisted in recruiting additional staff to carry out the new functions, which also included producing and printing union material such as the monthly paper, *Liberty*. Tom McCarthy, the Education and Training Officer, decided to create new posts for industrial relations tutors to be drawn from experienced staff, who he trained to a high standard, for teaching and mentoring shop stewards, branch committee members, full-time and part-time branch secretaries, activists and newly recruited staff.

Des Geraghty applied for one of the tutor posts and was delighted to be accepted and to be able to combine his trade union activity with important educational work, something he now considered vital for the advancement of trade union competencies and values. He loved the work, although it did require a lot of travel and time away from home during union courses, which rapidly increased in popularity and were soon held in all parts of the country.

Des also became keenly aware of the general low level of participation by female members in the union organisation and he saw the urgent need to increase their access to education and training activity at all levels. It was also evident that the union's low-paid and low-skilled workers, so many of them women, were the most vulnerable in the rapidly changing world of work in the country. This clearly needed a much wider focus on training and skill development for workers in their individual employments – much wider than shop steward training for industrial relations activity alone.

The years 1974 to 1978 were particularly important ones for the ITGWU's development of initiatives involving the integration of social and economic policies and workers' education, training and develop-ment. Various interesting initiatives were developed during those years, by members of the union's Research and Education and Training departments – one of them with the words of The Beatles ringing in their ears:

Help me if you can, I'm feeling down,
Help me get my feet back on the ground -
Oh please, please help me ...

This became the slogan for the union's HELP campaign – Higher Earnings for the Lower Paid. The campaign focused on a range of issues that would improve the status and earnings of lower-paid workers and was drawn up by Des Geraghty in the Education and Training Department and Rosheen Callender in the Research Department. It was launched at the union's 1978 Annual Delegate Conference, along with two other important discussion papers prepared by the Research Department – one on wages and economic policy, by Manus O'Ri-ordan and the other on social policy, by Rosheen Callender.

The HELP campaign argued for a move away from the purely percentage pay increases which had characterised previous National Wage Agreements, to a fixed sum plus a percentage. This would be much more beneficial to the lower-paid workers, most of them women, than simple percentage increases, as would improvements in the tax and social welfare codes for the lower paid.

Other issues raised at that time were productivity bargaining rather than extra overtime, equal pay for work of equal value and on-the-job training and upskilling in many more employments. This broader approach was later adopted by FÁS as their One-Step-Up training policy, in order to encourage employers and workers to develop improved job opportunities and progression for existing employees. Historically, craft workers and general workers were separated by the apprenticeship system, which created a barrier to adults seeking to upskill at various stages of their working life. Education and training for both skilled and unskilled workers was seen as the best approach to overcoming these distinctions, as was the policy of embracing new technologies and better forms of work organisation. Pension and sick pay schemes, often applied only to clerical and administrative workers, were recognised as major benefits requiring serious attention for manual and less skilled grades, as were workplace health and safety improvements.

Reductions in the tax burden, especially for lower-paid workers, was to become an important issue for national bargaining and union representations to successive governments. It was evident that the value of small pay increases could be quickly eroded by the tax and PRSI system, if the true value of the increases were not accompanied by complementary adjustments in the PAYE system. This important departure from the 'bread alone' approach to employment was an adoption and expansion of the 'Bread and Roses' theme of the Lawrence women of 1912. The spirit of James Oppenheim, in his 1911 song for the women workers, was now finding expression in the adoption of the social wage as the objective, the broader vision of a fairer and more equitable world of work for both men and women:

> *As we go marching, marching, we battle too for men,*
> *For they are women's children and we mother them again,*
> *Our lives shall not be sweated from birth until life closes,*
> *Hearts starve as well as bodies;*
> *Give us bread but give us roses.*

It was a progressive direction, reflected increasingly in the policies of individual unions and also within the ICTU. The need for proper work–life balance, dignity, respect and safety at work, were important requirements for adaptation to new technologies and progressive change in most employments. In time, the employers recognised that good standards of employment were a *sine qua non* for successful enterprises and for the retention of quality staff; and broadly accepted the changes proposed by the trade unions.

Our membership of the European Economic Community (EEC) also brought a major advance for all workers, and women in particular, as Ireland was obliged to adopt higher standards of social policy and, particularly, to implement legislation to guarantee equal pay for equal work and work of equal value. Although most trade unions opposed membership of the EEC in the first referendum, mainly because of sovereignty fears, very soon the economic and social benefits of Europe were recognised as beneficial and membership of the European project was more generally accepted. Although there were many aspects of the European project requiring continued improvements for workers it was evident that future progress could best be achieved by active participation in the EEC.

Des and many others now recognised that economic analysis had to move from uni-dimensional calculations based on supply and demand, competitive markets and bottom-line results to a much more multi-dimensional science that could properly calculate and embrace all the economic, social and environmental consequences that flow from economic activity. So many apparently desirable and currently profitable activities were demonstrably damaging people's health and welfare and rapidly destroying the natural order. He knew we had to learn how to make all the calculations necessary to help us understand how to deliver a 'just transition' to a more sustainable future.

In the past these issues were important but now they are essential if we are to have a future. Society will have to treat domestic and international markets more as valuable servants of humanity rather than the dominant, all-pervasive master of our destiny. Indeed, far greater co-operation between people, nationalities and economies is clearly a more urgent priority than any *laissez-faire* competition practices, if our species is to have a serious chance of survival in the decades ahead. The recent OECD multilateral agreement on the taxation of multinationals is a small start but other areas of co-operation are needed to address the issue of climate change. By now, it should be clear to all that a more radical approach to co-operation for global health and climate change are absolutely essential.

14

Gael Force Winds

When John F. Kennedy was visiting Ireland in 1963, three of the Geraghty brothers were on their way to a meeting for the establishment of an organisation in Dublin. It was called Scéim na gCeardchumann – a Trade Union Scheme. They were going to meet Cristóir De Baróid from Cork, where the organisation had existed for some years. Essentially, the creation of this organisation in Dublin was intended to bring together trade unionists to explore their history, traditions, culture and language. Sé, Des and Hugh had an interest in all these subjects and welcomed the idea of being part of such a new organisation.

There was a strong Cork contingent on the initial committee, including Barry Desmond of the ICTU, Michael O'Leary, then a newly elected Labour TD, and Tony Coughlan from Trinity College, Dublin. Also included were Tomás Mac Gabhann from Gael Linn, Ned Stapleton, a traditional musician and strong republican, and Máirín Johnson from the Liberties, a singer and folklorist and member of the Labour Party. Packie Early, a radical member of the carpenters' union, and Micheál Ó Ghríofa, a Connemara man and headmaster of Scoil Lorcáin, an all-Irish school in Monkstown, were also on the committee. Des Geraghty, initially a member of the committee, succeeded Michael O'Leary as the organisation's secretary in 1964.

Free Irish language classes were established for workers in a number of union premises with the support of Seamus O'Toole, Seán

O'Laoighin, Ruairí O'Tuairisg and Gearóid O'Cruadhlaoie, who all gave their teaching services free of charge. Two of the pupils who attended those classes, when they could make it, were Luke Kelly and his brother Jimmy. A series of lectures on economic, social and political issues were also organised, which included such speakers as Jim Kemmy from Limerick, a member of the Bricklayers' Union; Martin O'Donoghue, an economist and later a Fianna Fáil minister; Mattie O'Neill of the ITGWU; Máirtín Ó Cadhain and many others with interesting views on current affairs. Increasingly, the membership became actively involved in many of the progressive campaigns of that time.

Over time, historic trips were organised, as well as regular hiking expeditions in the Dublin and Wicklow mountains. Dancing and music were provided for in a series of oícheannta chaidrimh (social evenings), where a great variety of music, céilí/set dancing took place – at a time when set dancing wasn't approved by the 'official Gaeilgeoirí' of the Gaelic League, but the Scéim had no such objections. Traditional seannós, accompanied singing and Irish conversation were all encouraged. Some of these very popular events took place in the Clarence Hotel or in the Bricklayers' Hall on Cuffe Street. Seán Keane of the Chieftains recently told Des that his first date with his wife Marie took place at one of those events in the Bricklayers' Hall. Mick O'Connor and the members of the Castle Céilí Band were great supporters, as were other musicians such as Barney McKenna, Michael Tubridy and the O'Reilly family from Cavan and Dublin.

Later, the annual Connolly Concert was organised in Liberty Hall, at which many notable musicians performed over the years – The Dubliners, Al O'Donnell, The Press Gang, The McKennas, The Ludlows, The Green Linnets, Shay Healy, Seosamh Ó hÉanaí, Leo Rowsome ('the King of the Pipers'), Cathleen Maude, Máirín Johnson, Festy Conlon and Seán Ó Conaire (known as '007') and many more. Des frequently acted as 'fear a' tí' for these concerts. The proceeds of these concerts provided the basic funding for the Scéim as all these entertainers gave their services free.

Later in the decade, Deasún Breatnach and the Scéim organised a co-op to assist the small Gaeltacht of Rath Cairn in County Meath by marketing and distributing sacks of potatoes in Dublin, grown by the people of the Gaeltacht. Rath Cairn was a neglected area, full of great people, that had been established as part of a government scheme to transplant families from the congested Gaeltacht areas in the west to the Midlands. Unfortunately, there was a complete lack of facilities in Rath Cairn, with no local employment for the people and only a small national school in this new Gaeltacht. It only got recognition as a Gaeltacht after a major campaign by the community and with national support. As a consequence, many of the recent arrivals had to emigrate to find work in Britain, or commute to Dublin for employment on the building sites in the city.

The Geraghty brothers' emphasis on culture was part of their belief that Irish cultural activity had often been denied to workers because of prohibitive costs and various forms of class distinction. The Irish language in Dublin tended to be monopolised by very conservative elites, or by civil servants and middle-class professionals, who did not always encourage wider participation in their activities by the lower orders. Brendan Behan had a blast at these people in his harsh poem in Gaelic, 'An Rannaire' ('The Versemaker') in which he described them as puerile pioneers and 'Gach duine acu críochnúil cúramach cráifeach' (each one of them completely careful and devout). Myles na gCopaleen too took a similar swipe at them in his book *An Béal Bocht – The Poor Mouth*.

Scéim membership was drawn from very diverse backgrounds: it was considered an open and non-dogmatic organisation of the left. This attracted the support of young people of various political tendencies, who were willing to support and participate in promoting good progressive causes. As the revolutionary 1960s developed, members became increasingly involved in housing action, anti-apartheid marches and pickets, civil rights demos, supporting industrial disputes and joining in Irish language protests. Later in the 1960s Des and others participated in the Northern Ireland Civil Rights Association marches in such places as Derry, Armagh and Newry. He also attended meetings of the students of the People's Democracy in Saint Mary's Hall in Belfast.

Séamus and Hugh were both loyal members and participants in the Scéim's activities. Sé was a born raconteur and from an early age was a lover of classical music. He never missed an opportunity to get to all the operas in the Gaiety with his mother, Lily, who shared his passion for opera, as well as a love of Irish music and song. Sé was familiar with all the popular operas, loved the arias and choruses and became an authority on great singers from Caruso to Margaret Burke Sheridan. He also had a very special regard for Seán Ó Riada and his music. But Sé was essentially a visual artist at heart. He spent a considerable part of his youth in the National Art Gallery, and he could tell you where any important painting was on display. At an early age, he was accepted into the National College of Art, where he displayed a lot of early promise. Unfortunately, he gave up his ambition in the art world and like his brothers took up employment as a trade union official. He served for a time as branch secretary for the ATGWU in Waterford, where he made a considerable impact on the industrial relations of that city.

However, Sé's heart was always in Dublin and it wasn't long before he withdrew from the union in Waterford to return to Dublin and take up employment as a law searcher, genealogist and occasional book dealer. Like others before him, his fondness for books meant that he had a stronger preference for keeping his books than selling them, and he ended up with a large and very valuable book collection. In law searching, Sé developed an encyclopaedic knowledge of virtually every notable property in Dublin. He knew the detailed history of their origins, owners and styles; when streets were built, who built them, and every associated road, lane and back alley north or south of the Liffey. There was nothing he loved better than imparting his vast knowledge of the city and its many peculiarities to those who wanted to know. His particular focus was often on the stories behind the buildings: the greed and avarice of the landlords, how they treated their staff and tenants and their ownership of large estates in rural Ireland.

Over his lifetime, Sé managed to accumulate an enormous collection of books and historic documents, which he eventually bequeathed to the Ballyfermot Library. He also gave a detailed history of Lord

Leitrim and his estate management to a special library in Carrick-on-Shannon. More than anything else, though, Sé loved to socialise in the old city pubs and he had a regular corner barstool in Neary's Pub of Chatham Street, suitably close to the back of the Gaiety Theatre. Sé himself was also known, on occasions, to burst out singing an aria or two, whenever the circumstances allowed for such spontaneous joviality. The Scéim was just the place for his creativity and participation.

The focus of the left-wing Scéim on Irish language and culture may seem strange in retrospect, as the establishment and state-funded language movements were all too often associated with conservatism and national isolationism. In fact, the Irish language was, and is, as much a victim of the lost aspiration for a progressive Irish republic as anything else. Over the decades, the native speakers of the Gaeltacht were allowed to depart from the country, almost unnoticed, as labourers and low-skilled migrant labour for the construction sites of Britain and America. After decades of self-government and a questionable independence, there were few of the 'comely maidens' of de Valera's imagination left to dance at the crossroads. The pride and self-confidence of the Gaeltacht was sapped by emigration but sustained by the determination of the people, in spite of their economic circumstances.

It took the Coiste Cearta Sibhialta na Gaeltachta (Gaeltacht Civil Rights) of the 1960s to awaken the political establishment to the actual needs, as yet not fully understood, of the people who were trying to eke out a decent living in the Gaeltacht areas, primarily in the west of the country. Neither did the establishment give much practical support to those who chose to use the language in the country or abroad. The wisdom of an Irish seanfhocal could well be applied in this case: 'Ní thuigeann an sách an seang' (the well-nourished don't understand the needy).

Des firmly believed that everyone born in Ireland, or who chose to live in the country, was the beneficiary of an immeasurably rich cultural heritage of language, literature and poetry, in both the Irish and the English language; a unique musical tradition of national and international value; a community with strong communitarian values; and a rich and beautiful land with an environment worthy of preservation and enhancement. He knew we had a valuable inherited wealth that money could never buy, and whose loss would be an enormous tragedy. Des also believed that this inheritance is something open for all to share, and we should never allow it to be taken from us by neglect.

One of the most solid and reliable members of the Scéim from its foundation was Hugh Geraghty, the youngest of the brothers. He was involved in many organisations and was a trusted treasurer, secretary or chair of several. For example, he was Chair of the Crumlin Centre for the Unemployed for a number of years. Just two years before his early death in 2007, at the age of only 61, he also became President of the Irish Labour History Society. Hugh had railways and history in his blood; he served an apprenticeship as a fitter-turner in the CIÉ Inchicore Rail Works and worked there for 25 years. He followed that as an official in the ICTU, where he spent 13 years as Secretary of the CIÉ Group of Unions, an area often filled with intense conflict and complex industrial relations activity. Hugh had a reputation for absolute integrity and honesty in all his dealings with workers and management. Management and workers installed a bench outside Inchicore railway works to commemorate his contribution to all those who worked there.

One of the movements supported by members of the Scéim was the 'Defence of the West', promoted by Peadar O'Donnell, Packie Early and Dónal Donnelly. It was a self-help movement encouraging communities and groups in the west of Ireland to defend their communities from unemployment and emigration through increased co-operation and improved social organisation. The most noteworthy example of Defence of the West activity took place in Glencolmcille in Donegal, under the energetic direction of Fr McDwyer. Volunteers from Dublin and elsewhere took part in regular voluntary work camps. Hugh Geraghty, along with Jim Monaghan and many others, were very active in the Glencolmcille work camps. Others involved in that national campaign for the survival of beleaguered rural communities were Eithne McManus, now Eithne Viney, together with Michael Viney, who worked for the *Irish Times*.

Community-led projects increased along the western seaboard where communities rediscovered the traditional concept of the

meitheal, a communal work party, and comhar na gcomharsan (co-operation of neighbours), to stem the raging tide of emigration. For a
time local self-help projects flourished in many isolated communities
in the west, bringing new hope to the surviving families who lived
there.

Hugh also made an invaluable contribution to the history of Irish
labour with his history of William Partridge, which renewed an awareness of this remarkable Citizen Army man. Partridge died in 1917, a
short time after his 1916 involvement in the College of Surgeons garrison
with Michael Mallin and Constance Markievicz. William Partridge
was born in Sligo in 1874, and, like Hugh, was a railway fitter. He was
a member of the same union, originally the Amalgamated Society of
Engineers (ASE), which later became the Amalgamated Engineering
Union (the AEU). He was an early member of the Gaelic League and
Sinn Féin, a captain in the Irish Citizen Army and vice-president of
the Army Council. At the time of his death, Partridge was vice-president of the Dublin Council of Trade Unions and an elected Dublin
City councillor. He followed a path, through his working life, that was
not unlike that of Hugh himself; and as a consequence, this work on
Partridge was a true labour of love on Hugh's part. Pádraig Yeates, the
labour historian, wrote:

> *Hugh Geraghty's book has rescued an important pioneer of
> modern trade unionism and socialism from oblivion. During
> the 1913 lockout William Partridge was probably the most
> significant workers' leader after Larkin and Connolly and, as
> the author shows, more typical of the rank and file.*

Members of the Scéim had a role in the early formation of the Housing
Action Committee in the early 1960s. One afternoon, Des and a
friend, Paul Gleeson, were en route to the city via the South Circular
Road, when they were confronted by the exodus of a large, bedraggled
band of men, women and children from the Arthur Griffith Military
Barracks. They were pushing prams, carrying children, trying to hold
onto shoes and clothing and attempting to keep older children safe
from the passing traffic. In the midst of this group was Denis Dennehy

and his wife, Mary. Denis was known slightly to Des, who had come across him previously, but never in such pathetic and stressful circumstances. Des and Paul joined the small protest march into the city and learned from Denis that there had been a dispute in the barracks about the separation of families there – fathers from mothers and children – in emergency housing accommodation. These were all homeless families in dire need of shelter. They had been temporarily housed in the barracks, in what they considered to be inhuman conditions. They had decided to take to the streets to highlight their intolerable circumstances and Abbey Street corner was their proposed destination, where they planned to hold a public protest meeting. Unfortunately, however, they had no notion where they were going to sleep that night.

This protest group did draw some public attention but no immediate solution to their problems was evident. Des spoke at their meeting in support of their cause and called for support from the public for them, and also for the thousands of other homeless people sleeping rough in the city. After the meeting, they decided to camp out on Mountjoy Square. Des knew that there were some large Fianna tents in the Sinn Féin headquarters close by in Gardiner Place, and succeeded in getting their support in providing a temporary homeless encampment on the square.

This was followed by daily protest meetings which generated considerable support from civil liberties groups and, in particular, from Dr John O'Connell TD and Máirín de Búrca of Sinn Féin, a great campaigner for the poor and homeless of the city. Public commentators such as Proinsias Mac Aonghusa also gave support, which increased the pressure on Dublin Corporation to provide more acceptable emergency accommodation. The dilemma for the corporation was that the acute shortage of homes required it to operate a priority list system and it was understandably fearful of responding to any perceived 'queue jumping' by particular pressure groups.

As the weeks passed and frustration grew in the Mountjoy Square encampment, a plan was being hatched for some of the men to occupy Nelson's Pillar and hang a large protest banner, calling for housing, from the top platform of the monument. When John O'Connell TD became aware of this proposed illegal occupation, he set about securing mobile homes for the families. Gradually these particular families dispersed and that particular episode in the housing action campaign came to an end.

However, the seeds had been sown then, in the 1960s, for larger protests about housing needs in subsequent years. But like so many other important social issues, the housing problem remained with us – 'it hasn't gone away, you know'.

On 2 February 1965, a four-year contract, in which the Department of Local Government was directly involved, was signed for the planning, design and construction of the Ballymun housing scheme. This was to provide over three thousand housing units in system-built tower blocks. Some of the blocks were fifteen storeys high and it was hoped that a factory production facility would also be developed on site, to manufacture other components for future system-built housing projects. The scale of this four-year project was such that it was optimistically heralded as the solution to Dublin's social housing needs. The project served some purpose, but it proved not to be the ideal model for the future resolution of the city's housing needs. Des continued to feel, after decades of dealing with housing issues – as a campaigner, a trade union national industrial secretary for construction and later, as the chair of the Affordable Homes Partnership – that one clear conclusion was that simply building more and more housing units in working-class ghettos or high-rise towers was not the ideal solution.

He felt strongly that there was an absolute necessity for a future plan to construct and develop sustainable communities for mixed-income families, with homes of manageable human proportions, in suitable locations, at affordable prices. This would need to be supported by decent local public and private services. Building public housing on public lands had an important role to play, but was definitely not the complete answer to Ireland's housing needs. Markets can work for people with the money to participate in them but creating homes at an affordable price requires major public investment in diverse forms of suitable rental accommodation.

15

Women: Chains or Change?

In a family of five boys and their father, the concerns of women were rarely discussed. Yet Lily, their mother, was undoubtedly the dominant influence in their daily lives. She was the 'Mother of all the Geraghtys', a loving yet formidable character who feared no one and was a staunch defender of all her boys. She kept open house for family, friends and relatives, so the Geraghty home was always buzzing with life and conversation. Books were encouraged, as were music and song; and musicians and other 'oddballs' were always welcomed. In their home in Cornmarket, and later in Curlew Road in Drimnagh, people gathered to meet and exchange views, keep in touch, tell a tale or sing a song. It was usually a happy place and all the young boys had fond memories of their childhood days, at home, in school or on the street. Tom often remarked humorously that while none of them went to college, they did manage to meet the scholars.

Des was a very clingy child and when he was very young he never wanted to let his mother out of his sight. He would always object to her going out without him. For a long time he was not quite sure why that was the case, but realised later that he had been separated from her for a considerable time as a young child; he had been cared for by three female cousins and his aunt Maggie while Lily was extremely ill. Her condition was considered such that all the boys were farmed out for some time, to allow Tom to continue with his daily work duties.

While the cousins all made a great fuss of their baby cousin and he received the best of care, he had clearly developed a subconscious fear that his mother might disappear again.

As a consequence, on many evenings, Lily would allow Des to sit on the stairs of Winstanley House, Number 1–2 Cornmarket, watching her scrub the wooden stairs of the house from top to bottom, while the offices were closed and Tom was home from work minding the other boys. Des loved to accompany Lily on visits to local shops or dealers' stalls and never failed to be amazed by her facility for bargaining. He discovered that her mental arithmetic skills were such that no shopkeeper would ever dare add a penny to the price of a piece of meat for her. They would never be allowed to miscalculate her bill. Equally, no street dealer would get away with slipping damaged pieces of fruit or poor-quality vegetables into a paper bag. Lily knew where to get all the best bargains and would often walk a mile to save a few pennies and she would often time her visit to a fishmonger or butcher to catch them just as they were closing so that she could buy bits and scraps cheaply, capitalising on the shopkeeper's need to avoid storage or refrigeration of leftovers.

Lily's shrewd tactics meant that her meals were often made of pieces of meat or fish, such as Irish stew, a coddle of sausages and rasher scraps, or her own speciality, a red fish coddle. A dinner of cabbage and potatoes with scraps of bacon in the middle of the day would be followed that evening by a nutritious cabbage or onion soup. Another of Lily's specialities was hand-me-down clothes; and her hand-knitted jumpers, made after long hours of work, helped save the family costly visits to clothes shops. Des had nothing but admiration for Lily's household management skills and her ability to find money for all the family's needs. He learned a lot from her about hard work; in his view, if she had been the Minister for Finance, the finances of the state would have been in safe and capable hands. He knew also that in many working-class homes it was the women who did most of the grinding hard work and were the ones who kept families together in spite of all their financial difficulties.

Lily had a friend called Kitty Maher, a strong socialist, who was a retired cook. Kitty often visited the family in Cornmarket. She had worked in the MacBride house in Roebuck and in Lily's opinion, was the only one there with any serious politics.

On one occasion, when Des had just bought his first car, Lily asked him to bring her to visit an elderly relative in Ballinglen in County Wicklow. She was in the county home in Rathdrum at the time. He discovered that this relative had previously been the housekeeper in the home of Jack Yeats, the painter. She spoke Irish fluently and had a great love of folk tales and local history. Unfortunately, this fascinating old lady died just a few short weeks after their visit to Rathdrum.

Lily also knew Kathleen Behan, 'mother of all the Behans', and had fond memories of Countess Markevicz, the first-ever elected woman MP. She knew Helena Maloney, the radical trade unionist, as well as Madame Despard, the suffragist and rabid nationalist. Lily was, without the labels, an early women's liberationist and radical socialist who could always give as good as she got in any company. Herself and Tom never lost their Catholic faith, but would often argue that they kept the faith 'in spite of the clergy'.

From an early age, therefore, Des became fully conscious of the serious disadvantages faced by women in Irish society. They had no senior status in the Catholic Church – or any of the other Churches, for that matter. They were almost unmentioned in school history books; they held few senior positions of authority; and were generally compelled to work in lower-paid, insecure jobs. They were the dominant employees in shops and offices, working as clerks or typists; and in the catering services, as waitresses or cooks but rarely as managers or chefs; or in the health services as nurses or cleaners but not often as consultants; and in the community at large, usually as child minders.

While there were a small number of advances for women in the 1960s, it was not until the 1970s that the role and status of women received serious political attention in Ireland. We can thank our membership of the EEC for some of that; in particular, the Anti-Discrimination (Pay) Act 1974, which became effective on 31 December 1975, as required under an EEC Directive, entitled women to equal pay. Some progress on equal treatment in employment was also made when another EEC Directive was implemented by the 1977 Employment Equality Act.

However, full equal treatment in the social welfare system took much longer, due to piecemeal changes in the system even after the relevant Directive was supposed to have been implemented. In particular, successive governments baulked at paying thousands of married women equal treatment arrears that had accumulated due to the delays in fully implementing that Directive. After many years of campaigns and lobbying, the process was finally completed in 1996, under the three-party Rainbow government, thanks to the smallest of the parties, Democratic Left, making it an essential condition for entering government.

In 1969, Des married Mary Maher from Chicago, a journalist with the *Irish Times*. Their house on the North Strand soon became a regular gathering-place for women who were anxious to address the many inequalities affecting women in Irish society. Mary was a powerhouse of ideas and rationality, a very strong trade unionist and a proud Irish-American who felt at home in Ireland from the day she landed. She launched herself immediately into the growing debate and concerns about women's rights, which had not been well served in Ireland since the foundation of the State. She began to focus on these discriminations in the pages of the *Irish Times*, with the full support of the paper's deputy editor, Dónal Foley, and editor, Douglas Gageby.

One of the first women to engage in discussions with Mary about the equality agenda, in her home on the North Strand, was Máirín de Búrca, a vigorous local campaigner on many social issues. Des had been her election agent for the Dáil election at which she came very close to winning a seat. Later, in 1976, Máirín challenged the Juries Act, which had excluded most women from jury service. Justice Walsh ruled in Máirín's favour, on the grounds that the Act was unconstitutional, and stated that the Act was 'undisguisedly discriminatory on the grounds of sex only'.

Others who joined those discussions included Máirín Johnson, Moira Woods, Mary Cummins, Mary Anderson and Mary Kenny. More formal meetings were held later in Mrs Gaj's restaurant in Baggot Street, where they were joined by such other stalwarts as Nuala

Fennell, Marie McMahon, Nell McCafferty. This group became the nucleus of the Irish Women's Liberation Movement (IWLM), which in 1971 published a radical document entitled *Chains or Change?* It set out the basic issues affecting women which the IWLM considered to be in urgent need of attention, such as equal pay; equality before the law; equality in education; access to contraception; justice for deserted wives, widows and single parents; and 'One Family, One House'.

The group became extremely active in promoting the issues in the national media, at public meetings and seminars, in trade unions and through picketing the Dáil. They even made RTÉ's *Late Late Show* with Gay Byrne, after which a meeting in the Mansion House attracted over a thousand supporters. The inclusion of contraception as one of the issues brought an early rebuke from Archbishop John Charles McQuaid, still a major power in the land, who wrote in a letter that 'every action which proposed to make procreation impossible was in itself unlawful'. The IWLM argued that the prohibition of contraception was a violation of basic human rights under Article 19 of the UN's 1948 Universal Declaration of Human Rights.

After that, gender issues such as family planning, contraception, abortion, divorce, homosexuality and gay peoples' rights, all previously avoided in public discourse, became more open topics of conversation and debate in the political system and in the community. Family planning was a major demand. Women demanded open and legal access to contraception. The famous 'contraceptive train' in 1971, when members of the IWLM travelled to Belfast to buy contraceptives and bring them back to Dublin, not only exposed the ridiculous denial of women's access to contraceptives but also demonstrated that women were no longer afraid to assert their rights or to be treated as subservient second-class citizens in Ireland.

The first Commission on the Status of Women reported in 1972 and outlined the status of women in the Irish economy. It provided a wealth of information on the role of women in the workforce at that time. Other groups then emerged, such as the Women's Representative Council and later the Women's Political Association. In the trade union movement, women were becoming increasingly active on similar issues. The ITGWU and the ICTU developed a twelve-point Working Women's Charter, which included equality of opportunity, access to all levels of education, including apprenticeships, VEC training, and refresher courses for women re-entering the labour force.

That Charter also included equal treatment on fringe benefits like bonuses, sick pay and pensions, crèches and childcare provision. It included the statement, 'There should be a national minimum income to alleviate the problems of low pay'. It did not state a statutory minimum wage, a concept that was not universally welcomed in the trade union movement at the time, because it was feared by some that a minimum rate might become the maximum for many low-paid groups. Later, the focus shifted again, more towards the concept of a 'living wage' rather than a poverty level of minimum income, with the need for such important additional services as childcare at an affordable cost.

These proposals became part of the initial agenda of the Trade Union Women's Forum, which was formed in the mid-seventies. The TUWF comprised women from various unions who came together to encourage more women to join unions and increase women's participation at all levels of their organisations. The TUWF advocated trade union action to implement the many recommendations of various bodies, from the Commission on the Status of Women to the Irish Women's Liberation Movement to the many principles on women's equality set out in the various EEC Directives.

These included the complete removal of the marriage bar and marriage-differentiated pay scales, the introduction of paid maternity leave, the removal of all barriers to women's employment and promotion in specific areas, the banning of discriminatory job advertising and sex discrimination in pension schemes, and the provision of affordable childcare. Other important demands included the creation of permanent implementation machinery in the Labour Court and the Employment Equality Agency.

It's often not recognised that in the many years since the 1970s, right up to today, individual and group claims have had to be regularly pursued by trade unions in order to address these inequalities. Legislation helped to eliminate the most blatant sex discrimination, but it's a much slower process to fully eliminate all the other consequences of a long-standing culture of marginalisation and inequality.

One striking example of how long the elimination of some inequalities can take, even when required by legislation implementing a European Directive, was referred to earlier. This was the eventual payment of all social welfare equal treatment arrears to married women who had long been denied the same unemployment and other benefits as were paid to men. Despite protests about the 'excessive cost' of remedying this blatant injustice, payment was finally secured in 1996 by Proinsias De Rossa as Minister for Social Welfare, with Rosheen Callender of SIPTU working with him as his special adviser.

In the 1970s, Des and his colleagues in the ITGWU's Education and Training Department had included material on equality issues in their shop steward training courses. So also did the ICTU, which placed it, with many related demands, on its industrial relations agenda. This was facilitated subsequently by various national agreements and through national bargaining, on what became a broader agenda than that of the earlier wage agreements. Together with many of his colleagues, Des recognised the value of pursuing not only the traditional pay increases through local collective bargaining, but also developing a much wider national approach for improving the actual living standards for all workers and their families.

In the UK economy, the trade unions were generally confined to local or industrial bargaining on pay and workplace issues, while they would depend on a Labour government to implement any national improvements required through the political system. In Ireland, it was never possible to rely on the election of a Labour government to implement major advances on a broader trade union agenda, so national collective bargaining became the only available mechanism. Many of the UK-based unions have tended to become more sceptical about national bargaining over the years, but the purely Irish-based unions knew that national bargaining was their best bet for dealing with many issues requiring political or national action by employers.

In 1983, the TUWF published an interesting booklet on some of the main remaining issues for women at that time. It was called *Topical Issues for Women at Work* and had an article by Padraigín Ní Mhurchú of the Women Workers' Union, on the still-deficient rights of part-time workers. Another article was on 'Sex Discrimination in Social Welfare' by Eithne FitzGerald, an economist and Labour Party councillor at the time, which spelt out the remaining discrimination in that area. Another article was on the ban on women's night work which, amazingly, still persisted. It was by Patricia O'Donovan, lawyer and deputy legislative officer in the ICTU. Finally, there was an interesting article on 'Time versus Money' by Rosheen Callender, an economist and senior researcher in the ITGWU at that time. In that article, Rosheen raised issues about paid and unpaid work; the need to reorganise work on economic and social grounds; working hours, health and social services for women; and labour laws generally, especially as they affected women. She also called for the introduction of a national minimum wage, as this would be a tangible benefit for thousands of women on low pay who were not likely to ever benefit from equal pay legislation because they had no relevant male comparitors.

When the national minimum wage was finally introduced in 2000, it did more to raise women's average earnings than all the difficult years of taking equal pay cases since the 1975 Act came into force. The employers tried to delay this legislation and argued, as they had on equal pay, that it would result in job losses and be bad for our competitive economy. Neither these arguments, nor the fear that 'the minimum would become the maximum', ever proved to be valid objections.

When Mary Robinson was elected President of Ireland in 1990, following her nomination by the Labour Party and the Workers' Party, it was evident that something fundamental had changed in Ireland. It was as if the Republic had suddenly come of age. The women who had so often saved us, who had borne the brunt of our sorrows, who had carried our guilt and our suffering for generations, had finally come home. We were now closer to some degree of maturity as a democracy.

Mary Robinson, who had supported so many human rights causes, who had supported contraception, homosexual law reform and had marched against the destruction of Wood Quay, was the popular choice of the Irish people for President. She lived up to our expectations and more, changing the presidency from a symbolic institution to an active source of social and political transformation. She brought life and hope to forgotten communities, remembered the heartbreak of our emigrants, quoted the best of our poetry and made us proud to be Irish. Following her presidency, her leading human rights role in the United Nations and her global role in addressing climate change and related issues have continued to bring respect and prestige to her country.

Mary Robinson also laid the firm foundations upon which both subsequent presidents, Mary McAleese and Michael D. Higgins, could build our hopes even higher and make our achievements even greater in the eyes of the world. They have all shown us how to rise above the petty differences of the past; to hold out a hand of friendship across borders; and to chart a new and more progressive course for the future, not only for the people of Ireland but the world at large.

For the Geraghtys, the song 'Bread and Roses', about the factory women in Lawrence in 1912, was fulfilling its prediction that the rising of the women would raise us all up:

As we go marching, marching, we bring the greater days,
The rising of the women means the rising of the race;
No more the drudge and idler - ten that toil where one reposes,
But a sharing of life's glories -
Bread and roses, bread and roses.

16

Dear Harp of My Country, in Darkness I Found You...

'This music of ours possesses the power of magic. It can put us in touch with ourselves in ways no other art form can do. It can touch the pulse of ancestral memory, allowing us to redefine our dreams of what it is to be Irish. It can bring the lonely famine landscape to life, it can soothe the trauma and troubles of existence, it is possessed of the veiled eroticism of tenderness. It can adorn a moment of joy, it can sharpen a moment of sorrow. It is a gift of nature dispensed with the abandon of wildflowers' - the late Tony MacMahon

In the Geraghty household, Irish music and song was greatly appreciated and enjoyed. For them the singing and musical traditions of Ireland were never considered an exclusively rural phenomenon but a very live aspect of their urban life. Ballad singing was popular, and still is in many singing circles, in the cities where the street singers told their stories, remembered important events, or entertained with tales of love, sorrow or joy. Historic events and notable occasions were frequently recorded for posterity through a damn good song.

What is often less understood is that instrumental traditional music was sustained in the large cities, particularly Dublin, when it was in rapid retreat from many rural areas because of unrelenting emigration and rural depopulation. In rural communities musicians often had to contend with clerical disapproval as unsupervised house or crossroad dances or associated celebratory events were considered potential 'occasions of sin and debauchery.' This could be a particularly virulent condemnation when anyone present at such events might consider taking alcohol.

Traditional music was practised and passed on through particularly gifted families, played for special events such as house dances, wakes or weddings, and at a variety of celebratory occasions such as family gatherings considered to be occasions that merited special celebration. Professor Michael Cronin, Director of Literary and Cultural Translations at TCD, points out in his book *Irish and Ecology* that, 'contrary to modernist misconceptions about a land beholden to the theme music of the crossroads, for much of the 1920s, 1930s and in Irish broadcasting circles and beyond, there was a widespread bourgeois disdain for the music of the common people'.

Seán O' Casey, himself a one-time piper and Gaeilgeoir, took up this theme in 'Inishfallen Fare Thee Well', writing disdainfully:

> *When a host of Irish Harps was sounding 'Let Ireland Remember the Days of Old' at a mass meeting, the new politicians and people decided that they should become genteel, with really nice manners to show how fit for self-government they were ... the cruiseen lán was rejected for the cocktail glass ... the teachers of up-to-date and old world dancing were working night and day educating the vulgar hilarity of jig and reel from the joints of the adventists of the new aristocracy, so that grace and sweet easiness might take their place. Now it became a question of dignity and poise rather than one of enjoyment bred out of Gaelic prancing in the dances of the wilder Irish.*

The roots of Irish music are deeply embedded in Irish society, stretching back to very ancient times. As far back as the twelfth century Giraldus Cambrensis, Gerald of Wales, an eminent Welsh historian and archdeacon of Brecon, who wasn't exactly enamoured of the Irish people, said after a visit to this country that we were 'a filthy people wallowing in vice: yet in the cultivation of instrumental music I consider the proficiency of this people to be worthy of commendation, and in this their skill is beyond that of any nation I have seen'.

Archaeologists excavating in County Wicklow found a set of wooden pipes, thought to be a musical instrument from the early Bronze Age, dated between 2120 and 2085 BC. They are made of yew wood, which is the material of other wooden pipes dated 400 BC that were found in Killyfadda, County Tyrone, so we know that some form of music formed an important part of prehistoric life on this island.

William Congreve (1670–1729), the famous British playwright who studied in Kilkenny College and in Trinity College Dublin and was a close friend of Dean Swift, made the immortal and oft-quoted observation that 'Music has charms to soothe a savage breast, to soften the rocks, or bend a knotted oak'; and more recently the Ulster poet John Hewitt (1907–1987) described the native Irish as 'given to dancing and a kind of song seductive to the ear, a whining sorrow'.

Paddy Kavanagh, the Monaghan/ Dublin poet and author of 'Raglan Road', sung so brilliantly by Luke Kelly of the Dubliners, was obviously influenced by his father's music. He tells us in his poem 'A Christmas Childhood' that

> *My father played the melodion*
> *Outside at our gate;*
> *There were stars in the morning east*
> *And they danced to his music ...*
> *An old man passing said:*
> *'Can't he make it talk -*
> *The melodion.'*

Paddy's other very personal song, 'If Ever You Go to Dublin Town', is based on the air of an old city street song called 'Hand Me Down Me Petticoat' or 'She was a Quare One.'

Although we normally associate traditional music with dance music – reels, jigs, hornpipes, polkas, slides – it has a much broader and more varied range than that. In the early Celtic era they acknowledged three strands of music: the goltraí (laments); geantraí (light or happy music); and suantrí (lullabies). These categories were generally associated with the ancient harpers and feature prominently in Irish mythology and in the ancient stories.

Clan marches are another element of our musical heritage, generally played on pipes for marches into battle or on ceremonial occasions. Many of the early marches were later adapted to become dance tunes and would often be played for dancers. Another perhaps more classical element of our musical tradition is found in the beautiful compositions of Turlough O'Carolan, and the other harpers whose music was often played in the big houses for the Anglo-Irish gentry.

Another distinctive influence in our music is sean-nós singing, our ancient soul music. This tradition is still alive in the Gaeltacht areas and features prominently at the annual Oireachtas na nGaeilge. Most sean-nós songs come from the poetry of earlier Gaelic scholars and some come from church music, Gregorian chant, or hymns sung for religious rituals in the monastic settlements. Our indigenous music has absorbed many influences over the centuries and will no doubt continue to do so, as there are no inflexible boundaries that can curtail the development of a living musical tradition.

The Irish language and songs are interwoven in many of the rhythms and sounds and particular instruments have helped to produce its unique sound. Yet it's the individual performers who have determined the style and depth of the music and it's their skill that has helped bring this music alive for so many listening audiences. Because our music has roots in different regions of the country, a variety of local styles has emerged, often reflecting the nature of particular places, as well as the influence of particularly skilful local musicians.

For the poor travelling musicians, our early buskers, the poet Antoine Ó Raifteiri captures their circumstances in this short extract from his poem 'Mise Rafterí an File' ('I am Raftery the poet'):

Féach anois mé is mo chúl le balla,
ag seinnm ceoil do phócaí folamh.
(Look at me now with my back to the wall,
Playing music for pockets, with nothing at all.)

Particular families have played a major role in the preservation of our musical tradition and have passed it on from generation to generation. Over the past fifty years or so, many very talented groups have helped to expand the range and popularity of the music. The best of them have kept close to the genuine traditional sound of the music, making sure it's not totally sacrificed for purely commercial purposes. The acoustic instruments they use are often the most appropriate for reproducing the unique sounds of the tradition, if they are not totally obliterated by an overdose of intrusive percussion, electrification or drumbeating.

In Dublin and in particular in the Liberties the traditional music survived surprisingly well over the centuries. Leo Rowsome (1903–1970), the 'King of the Pipers', sustained an interest in uilleann piping by his playing, teaching and pipe-making. He taught piping in the Municipal School of Music from 1919 and was the driving force behind the Pipers' Club in Thomas Street over many decades. Having worked for fifty years in the Municipal School of Music, this master musician and purveyor of the Irish nation's treasury of piping never qualified for a pension, because he was only a part-time worker at the school.

Another pioneer, hardly remembered, was a Mrs Bridget Kenny, the mother of thirteen children. She died in 1915 at the age of fifty-nine in her home at 5 Madden's Court, off Thomas Street in the Liberties. She was described as 'Queen of the Irish Fiddlers' because of her remarkable talent as a musician. She was married to a piper named John Kenny and in the 1903 Oireachtas Fiddle Competition, three members of the family entered the contest. She was renowned for her ability and acknowledged by Colm O'Loughlin as the best fiddler of her time.

The national revival which grew from the closing decade of the nineteenth century brought the Gaelic League, the Feis Ceoil and the original Pipers' Club along with the Irish Literary Revival. In the early decades of the Free State, the survival of the music largely depended on a small number of enthusiasts who continued to play, teach and pass their skills on to the following generations.

From 1936 the Pipers' Club was a small faltering flame in the darkness, when traditional music and piping in particular were denied their rightful place in the cultural affairs of the state. While it was originally focused on the uilleann pipes, it later attracted many more musicians for its Saturday night sessions in 14 Thomas Street, the home of the 4th Battalion of the old IRA and the Old IRA Literary and Debating Society. City-based musicians were joined there by visiting musicians coming to the city or passing through on their way to and from England or the USA. Leo continued to teach the pipes in the club and through his teaching, broadcasting and concert performances kept the piping tradition alive and visible, at least to some extent, in the capital city.

Another smaller and lesser-known home of music was Saint Mary's music club in Church Street, over Lavin's pub and later in the old Boys' Brigade Hall a few doors away. John Egan, a Sligo flute player, was the central figure who attracted the finest fiddle and flute players to the weeknight sessions. While they were generally from the northwest, from Sligo, Leitrim or Mayo, many fine Dublin players also joined them, such as a young John Sheehan, later of Dubliners fame, who would be seen there performing his first tunes on the fiddle. Breandán Breathnach found the club a rich source of tunes for his important collection *Ceol Rince na hÉireann*. Des loved listening to the echo and reverberation of the timber flutes and fiddles in that old Georgian room and both the sound and the spirit of that music remained with him for ever after.

The advent of Seán Ó Riada, the composer and creative genius, with his Ceoltóirí Chualann, gave a great boost to the status and popularity of traditional music. Ó Riada was a talented composer and musician who brought a new dimension to the performance of traditional music. His great strength was his recognition of the individual styles of the musicians, allowing them to contribute individually to his varied arrangements of music sets. That was followed by the piper the late Paddy Moloney and his internationally famous group The Chieftains. The Dubliners brought an urban, Rabelaisian style and sharper edge to the tradition, with their street cred and their raw, vibrant approach.

The popularity of the Pipers' Club as a venue was part of an opening up of traditional music and song to a much wider audience in the late fifties and sixties. At one stage, the committee thought the club was in danger of being overwhelmed by beatniks or 'long-haired weirdos', so they introduced a ban on long hair. An early victim was Garech de Brún, a great supporter and lover of the music, who wore his hair in a ponytail. On one occasion, Barney McKenna was stopped at the door because he was dressed in a red shirt with a black lace tie. He had to lilt a reel to demonstrate his suitability for entry. The ban didn't last very long and soon people of all types and shapes were welcomed. One visitor was Ulick O'Connor, the poet and author, who certainly justified his welcome by writing the following poem, entitled 'The Pipers' Club':

The leaping finger tightens on the string,

Bow slips sideways in a sudden swoop;
The fiddler's found his air; with head in swing,
His glazed eyes ignore the captive group.
My knuckles whiten at my plight.
What silken word can match the fiddler's fling
Who saw a blackbird in a gap of light
And trapped its sweetness on a tightened string?

The brothers Des and Hugh attended regularly, with Des's close friend Mick O'Connor, the flute player, also from the Liberties. It was Mick who got Des to attend piping lessons in the Fintan Lalor Pipe Band beginners' classes and later to march and play the warpipes with the Adam and Eve's Boy Scout Pipe Band for St Patrick's Day.

Two other close friends were Seán Keane, later of the Chieftains, and his brother James, now in America. Both were remarkable musicians who had attended Francis Street CBS school and lived close to the Geraghty family in Drimnagh. John Keenan, who played the accordion, was a prominent member of the Pipers' Club and an old friend and neighbour of Lily O'Neill's relatives in Ballinglen in County Wicklow. A close friendship grew between Des and Barney McKenna, of Dubliners fame, both of whom were employed at the same time by the engineering branch of the Department of Posts and Telegraphs, supposedly providing telephones for the people.

Many other musical friendships developed in the Pipers' Club, with the O'Reilly family, the Potts family, the Rowsome family, fiddler Jim Christle, Jimmy Dowling, the piper and secretary of the club, and Paddy Bán O'Broin, Irish teacher, sean-nós dancer and flute player. Jim Nolan, the fear an tí, always ensured that 'a bird never flew on one wing' when getting a second song and knew when to bring on the heavy artillery when the accordions were invited to resume the session.

Out of the Pipers' Club grew the meeting in Mullingar at which Comhaltas Ceoltóirí Éireann was formed. It was the subsequent annual Fleadh Cheoil, organised in different counties, which allowed the opening up of the traditional music to all generations, players, dancers, listeners and local people. It was an important step on the road to a more open and mature Irish society, capable of experiencing enjoyment and fun, plenty of music, dance and song, without anyone's by your leave.

This was our Gathering of the Clans, a much improved version of the Donnybrook Fair, a poor people's Oireachtas, an improved Puck Fair (without a goat), an open-air céilí and a session of all sessions. The colourful arrival of the famous Clancy brothers to the Fleadh Cheoil in Ennis, in their báinín jumpers, was to copperfasten the American connection which has proved so rewarding for many musicians. The number of groups and individual performers has multiplied over recent years, bringing the music to far-flung quarters of the wider world.

The revival of set dancing was another advance from some of the ridiculous dancing rigidities of the past, allowing for a more natural engagement of men and women, more in tune with the gracious rhythms of the traditional music.

The Willie Clancy week in Clare is another important addition to the Fleadh Cheoil and has changed the emphasis of the assembly from competition to tutoring and informal performance. In Miltown Malbay, County Clare, this festival thrives on the musical tradition of the county, but it has also proved to be a musical mecca for the wider world. It has managed to assemble a team of top-class tutors and practitioners and has maintained the highest standards of performance. Clare is also blessed with first-class women concertina players following in the footsteps of the great Mrs Crotty of Cooraclare, who lived in Kilrush and brought the concertina into prominence in the late fifties on Ciarán Mac Mathúna's radio programmes. Tony McMahon, broadcaster and accordion player, also from County Clare, has been a powerful force in the preservation and promotion of traditional music. In recent years, in his collaborations with Steve Cooney and Barney McKenna, he also worked with Des and Rosheen in reviving the format of house concerts, through the Friendly Visit group, which organises intimate musical events in private homes.

These people and events have not only popularised the music but have also helped to liberate the inherited genius of the younger musicians and enhanced the attractiveness of the music in ways that now ensure its survival as an important Irish art form. While the ancient harps may be few in number on the city streets, there has also been a strong revival of harp-playing in more suitable places, as the ancient music escapes from the dark days of the past into the bright clear light of day.

Epilogue

On the Road to God Knows Where

However rocky our road has been for the last hundred years, the road ahead already looks decidedly rockier, with more twists and turns, highs and lows and, very likely, stormy weather and much poorer visibility. If Seán O'Casey's Joxer Daly thought the world was 'in a state of chassis' so long ago, a modern writer might find an even more derogatory word for it now.

Dr Ivor Browne, the eminent psychiatrist, in his book *Music and Madness*, describes it very well for me:

> *Our society is now like a boat on a river, drifting towards a waterfall. All around us the rapids are getting more turbulent but most of the occupants of the boat are behaving as if life is just flowing on as it always did. I feel we are now in a position where, unless all the warning signs are heeded and we make urgent efforts to reach the shore, our civilisation is going to be carried over the edge. We are in a race against time.*

Usually, I have found threats that create fear and insecurity to be bad medicine. But given the range of existential issues now facing humanity, it's difficult not to be fearful about the future and not to heed the good doctor's warning.

Being an eternal optimist, I have generally found hope and self-confidence a stronger medicine than fear for motivating people and inspiring them to face challenges with courage. Fear of eternal damnation has rarely stopped people sinning, but I am in no doubt that hope of a better life will inspire people to make major changes in their way of life. However, it is major change we require and not all of it can come from the 'little people' here or anywhere else. We have inherited a very unequal world and the vested interests who sustain that inequality are a serious obstacle to most of the major changes that we need to make.

If we embrace the idea of the environmental movement, 'think globally and act locally', we have an approach that can combine an awareness of the global changes that face the planet, and what governments need to do, with a call to action for each and every one of us. While the powers that be address the ozone layer and global warming, we all have to address the local sewer, the polluted river, the plastic litter, the packaging of our food and the food itself – everything about our way of life that contributes to these global problems.

Dean Swift, in one of his pearls of wisdom, pointed out one of our great follies when he wrote 'but in man we find the only creature, who led by folly, fights with nature.' Now we have to give up that fight and establish a new and more fruitful relationship with the natural world around us.

When speaking to people about the Irish language and its significance, I often invite them to start by considering the name of where they live and begin from there to learn more about the place they inhabit. That is often the pathway to a greater sense of place, an understanding of our wondrous heritage, our two languages, both a bit 'foreign', according to Brendan Behan; and all the physical and intellectual gifts we have inherited by living here. Then the people, the trees, the birds, the bees, the animals around us, the air we breathe and the water we drink become both valued gifts to be enjoyed and a source of constant wonderment.

I love Wordsworth's gentle words about looking and listening to nature: 'I have learned to look on nature, not in the hour of thoughtless

youth, but hearing oftentimes, the sad still music of humanity.' Padraig
Pearse had another sad observation on nature:

> *The beauty of this world hath made me sad,*
> *This beauty that will pass.*

One of the big issues of our time is migration. Clearly, given the
unstable nature of the world, it will continue to require more and
more attention by all the countries in the developed world. It will
continue to demand a generous response from Ireland and a much
more integrated European policy response in the future. Attitudes
in Ireland to migrants have improved slowly over recent years, as the
majority of our people learn the value that the new arrivals actually
bring to our community.

I have found from experience that people who truly value our
country, with all its differences, are well able to accept others and
readily learn to accommodate them as a new and valuable element in
our society. In the same way, I have found that people who choose to
live and work here often place a much greater value on all things Irish
than those who were born here and take it for granted. Equally, those
with a self-confidence about their own culture and identity have less
difficulty accepting those with a different culture as they don't feel
threatened by them.

It's difficult for me to conceive how a society driven by personal
greed, competition and exploitation can make all the necessary
changes that we are now faced with. We certainly need to find ways
to increase co-operation, far more than competition, in every aspect of
society and particularly in international affairs.

We need greater emphasis on social justice and genuine equality if
tackling climate change is to be accompanied with a real, rather than
a fictional, just transition. I believe that will require more effective
national and international structures, not alone on climate change but
on people change and all that that requires. That could be a real challenge for all of us but particularly for dealing with the powerful vested
interests who have such a major stake in maintaining the status quo.

Below the political system in Ireland I would like to see a new version of the meitheal oibre (a co-operative work party of neighbours), a structure akin to the national partnership, which would bring together all the major players in the economy and in society to thrash out the issues and actions requiring their attention. To overcome any fears of transparency and accountability at that level, a dedicated minister and an Oireachtas committee could exercise oversight over the conclusions of such a meitheal.

For us to counteract the divisive and reactionary nature of Brexit as time passes, we now require far more, not less, engagement with the people of Britain, Scotland, Wales and Northern Ireland. The consequences of Brexit are not simply about the single market or any trade border down the Irish Sea, but about all the progress and common purpose that membership of the European Union has given us. We could base our approach on the Scandinavian co-operation model, which predates the EU and could prove to be widely supported, without compromising any of our existing EU relationships. As part of this approach, a strong emphasis is also needed on non-governmental organisations (NGOs), on education and on culture; this could help to develop greater understanding and more shared aspirations, without immediately threatening anyone's political identity. An emphasis on NGOs could help us to minimise the often destructive nature of deep-rooted past enmities based on religious or political beliefs.

On the issue of identity, we can learn to recognise that we can all carry and respect multiple identities. Being born in Ireland or choosing to live in Ireland gives us all an Irish identity, while political choices can give us different identities without repudiating our place of origin. Our religion, class, language, colour, accent, sport, gender, age or choice of music are all part of a complex jigsaw of identity pieces, which may be different but, when put together, can also create a single picture.

In the future, national identity may not be the most valuable one for the survival of our species. It may not be as valuable as our human identity, which emphasises our need for a better relationship with the earth we inhabit as human beings. I like the integrity of the declaration by John Hewitt, the Ulster poet, about his own personal identity:

I'm an Ulster man of planter stock. I was born on the island of Ireland, so secondarily I'm an Irishman. I was born in the English archipelago and English is my native tongue, so I am British. The British archipelago are offshore islands to the continent of Europe, so I am European. This is my hierarchy of values and as far as I am concerned any who omits one step in that sequence of values, is falsifying the situation.

Having retained a personal hope that one day the people of this island will manage to throw off all the historic shackles of our conquest and devise way of living together as good neighbours and good Europeans, I want no borders, north–south or east–west, to keep us apart. However, I firmly believe that a rush with undue haste to a border poll in Ireland could do more to divide than unite us. We should remember how the Government of Ireland Act did that in 1921 and how the unfortunate departure from a relatively peaceful campaign for civil rights in the early seventies to a military campaign very soon afterwards drove us further apart for thirty years.

I see great merit in a truth and reconciliation process or some equivalent to address the hurt and enmity between the communities in Northern Ireland that require some means for a genuine healing. Such a process, if carefully handled, could help families to find common cause in sharing their grief and bitterness. Since the political system seems unable to achieve this is there not scope for the non-government, voluntary sector, community groups and trade unions to co-operate in such a process? There should no need for any Catholic–Protestant enmity anymore, nor is there any rational basis for enmity between other religions or beliefs, be they Christian, Muslim, Hindu, Buddhist, Jewish or Humanist, in a modern democratic Ireland. States based on a belief that a particular religion has a monopoly of truth and a special entitlement to power and control of a society always result in inequality and discrimination. We should, however, recognise that religious or other belief is a democratic choice for all, although it has all too often been used to disguise the power and privilege of some at the expense of others. Clearly, in my view, we have much more to do in relation to increasing co-operation between communities and developing mutual understanding on this island before a mere poll could hope to produce any viable form of unity.

We also have a lot more radical work to do to house our people at affordable prices, something which requires far more sophisticated planning, clearer differentiation of needs and separate forms of market regulation. Affordable homes and communities are much more than market commodities, and require to be separated from the 'housing market', which is about traded commodities and investment decisions. The housing ladder is a very slippery device and should not be the dominant concept. Public provision of rented accommodation is now the most pressing requirement for ending the homes crisis. Housing Travellers and migrants are also issues requiring sensitive handling which should be done in consultation with those directly involved. We will also have the added need for more accommodation to deal with new migrants, whether from Afghanistan or elsewhere, as well as the long-delayed reform and ultimate abolition of the direct provision arrangements. We also have public health needs and drug problems to address, along with all the many other day-to-day needs of people in our community.

Not being a great fan of neo-liberal capitalism, I have long believed that the future of humanity and our country actually requires a complete departure from a uni-dimensional market-driven form of economics based on personal or corporate profit-taking, to a more multi-dimensional economics based firmly on more solid economic, social and environmental accounting. I also support the tepid, though important, recent moves to make the multinational corporations pay higher minimum taxes by international rather than purely national agreement. I do understand the Irish government's need to ensure that larger countries do not simply shift that taxation from smaller to larger countries. Something worth considering might be a method for them contributing more to the European budget, or UN agencies, thus enabling a fairer distribution of resources to those who need it most.

I believe also that there is increasing scope in all societies for much more not-for-profit-type enterprise, encouraging more ethical and more environmentally friendly investment, with profits being recycled to address the needs of all stakeholders, rather than only those of the individual or institutional shareholders. Although I know that's not a new idea, it still seems too utopian a concept to be taken seriously for perhaps another hundred years. But if not, will there still be anyone here, at that stage, to implement such a radical concept?

We have achieved a lot in the last hundred years to give us some hope as we face the challenges of the next hundred. After all our travails, this is not a bad little country and we are no mean people, despite all the historic baggage we carry. But we have many more hills to climb, more sharp corners to navigate and a lot more energy to expend, if we are to achieve Seamus Heaney's 'Republic of Conscience' as an integral part of that Island of Equals that our family of seven – and so many others – 'dare to dream of'.

Barney McKenna –
In Memory of a Dubliner

From Royal Meath the noble minstrels fled,
with sundered harp and furtive thread,
exiled to wander through a land of tears,
sad melodies to whisper across the years.

Nothing left to save but a native pride,
song and verse of an ancient tribe,
music gleaned from the wailing wind,
the crash of waves and the march of time.

When in Dublin city new hope revived,
pipers and fiddlers fine music plied,
strings were twanged in more vigorous ways,
when McKenna his inspired banjo played.

Irish hearts could again now beat,
to rebel rhythms rising from the deep,
with nimble fingers and a spirit rare,
Barney's music rang out on the heady air.

To many well-worn songs a new life he gave,
rolling tuneful notes in wondrous waves,
like sunlight glancing on dark sullen streams,
found gold and silver riches, beyond our dreams.

An unscheduled journey thus began,
with Ronnie, Luke, Ciarán and John,
leaves blown together from different trees,
mingled on the crest of a Rabelaisian breeze.

Now his head he's laid down, perchance to dream,
of a timeless place, where ever his heart has been,
where the rarest of music, his spirit may play,
For the wind and the waves, to dance on the sea.

Des Geraghty, 2012